Out of the Closet
and Into the Light

Carol:

What a joy and
Blessing to meet you.
Hope my book will be
a help to you in your
walk with God. You are a
Gift from God to people
like me.

Rv. Jerry Stephenson D
(In Christ)

Out of the Closet and Into the Light

Clearing up the Myths and Giving Answers About Gays and Lesbians

Rev. Jerry Stephenson, TH.D., Ph.D.
Ex-Southern Baptist Minister

Writers Club Press
New York Lincoln Shanghai

Out of the Closet and Into the Light
Clearing up the Myths and Giving Answers About
Gays and Lesbians

Writers Club Press
an imprint of iUniverse, Inc.

For information address:
iUniverse
2021 Pine Lake Road, Suite 100
Lincoln, NE 68512
www.iuniverse.com

ISBN: 0-595-14551-5

Printed in the United States of America

Contents

Introduction

The issue of homosexuality has become a growing issue over the last few years. The subject is gaining new heights as gays and lesbians come out of the closet. This is true, especially among the famous that are coming out of the closet and saying they are gay and proud of who they are. It is those coming out of the closet all across the world which is making the difference. In this book we will look at past, present and future studies regarding homosexuality. In doing so, we are realizing how much we do not know about human sexuality. Homosexuality and heterosexuality are both complex, but we are making strides to understand their dynamics. The chapters ahead will show us how much some groups lack knowledge in the area of sexuality. Hopefully, this book will help those who are struggling with their orientation. Secondly, to help educate and guide family and friends of gays and lesbians. Thirdly, to help inform people of the misconceptions about gays and lesbians. Fourthly, to give the facts about gays and lesbians. In this book we will be focusing upon those Christian churches throughout history who have sought to tear down certain groups using the Bible as their whipping post. Therefore, it is not shocking that homosexuals are their focus today. We will look at the bigotry, hatred, lies, stupidity and ignorance coming out of such groups. Unfortunately, their message regarding homosexuality causes lasting scars for gays, lesbians, family and friends. Certain Christian churches continue to misinform people about homosexuality. It is this type of misinforming which causes psychological, mental, social and spiritual pain for all those involved. The reason for this book is due to the current debate on homosexuality and gay rights in the home, school, church and workplace. This book will shed light on the positive and truthful aspects of homosexuality. Hopefully, the chapters will bring hope and healing to all those who read its pages. If you are one of those who has been misinformed about homosexuality, then you will not want to miss reading this book. Unfortunately, there are those who are not about truth, but continue to spread their hate and bigotry about gays and lesbians. Those who are willing to seek truth with an open mind will find it. We will seek to find the truth regarding gays and lesbians by answering the misconceived ideas about homosexuality. It is only through understanding that one finds the freedom of truth. It is ignorance which brings about fear and hatred. Education is the key to ignorance. Also, education is the key to understanding those things you do not understand. There are many people out there who do not understand homosexuality, nor do they understand their own sexuality. The issues of homosexuality have now come to the forefront. The fact that gays and lesbians have been around since the written page is nothing new. It is only now that gays and lesbians break the silence of their closets and come out into the light. It is only now that gays and lesbians are finding the courage to stand up for their freedom and be who they are without regards to the harsh consequences some face. It is important to know that such groups like gays and lesbians bring about the reality of what freedom will cost a person. Gays and lesbians are your neighbor your parents, children or co-workers. They are doctors, lawyers, policemen, teachers and psychologists, ministers and the list goes on. Their history has helped make this world a better place to live. This book will help to bring hope and healing to all God's children. Chris Glaser best notes the conflicts which bring about psychological and spiritual ramifications:

Christian bodies are still wrangling acrimoniously over the acceptance of gay people as clergy or even as members of the church. Other minorities have fought oppression by Christian society: Jews, African Americans and Women. In each of these cases the establishment used religious claims to justify inequality or injustice and the churches were often among the last organizations to respond to reform (p. XIV, *Uncommon Calling*).

Unfortunately, we will never rid the conflicts of bigotry and hatred towards minority groups. But we have seen that throughout history time can heal some wounds. For example, African Americans still suffer from bigotry and hatred. The steps forward are sometimes slow coming.

Members of the Southern Baptist Convention, America's largest Protestant denomination and one founded in large part in the defense of slavery, voted overwhelmingly on Tuesday to apologize to African Americans for condoning racism for most of its history. In their resolution on racial reconciliation, the Baptists "repent of racism of which we have been guilty" and apologize to and ask forgiveness from "all African Americans" (p 13A, *The New York Times*).

The basis of their racism was built upon their misconceived beliefs found in the Bible regarding black people. This has always been their tactics to those things of which they simply have no knowledge. Someday the gay and lesbian community hopes to hear those same apologies from the Southern Baptist and any other groups, which sought to oppress them in any way. We cannot allow such behavior to continue in today's world. This book seeks to set the record straight. As we look at bigotry (homophobia) on many levels we will see the damage it causes. But in the end, may this book bring about psychological and spiritual healing of homosexuals, their families and friends.

Chapter 1

Homosexuality and Religion

In this chapter, we will be looking at Christianity in light of homosexuality. The history of Christianity is full of bigotry and hatred towards certain groups such as blacks, Jews, women and now homosexuals. This is not to say that Christianity is the only group out there who shows bigotry and hatred towards such groups as just was mentioned. But it is the radical Christian Movement that is speaking so loud today towards gays and lesbians. It is nothing new that certain Christian groups have gone to the Bible to preach their bigotry and hatred towards groups they did not know or hated. This chapter will focus upon the leadership of such Christian groups that have led the way for bigotry and hatred towards homosexuals. It is their ignorance and stupidity that affects those around them in the church and the non-churched alike. The Judeo-Christian tradition has a very narrow and unhealthy view of sexuality, especially in the area of homosexuality. This thinking was not always a part of Christian history—in John Boswell's book, *Christianity, Social Tolerance, and Homosexuality*, argues for many centuries Catholic Europe showed no hostility towards homosexuality.

Between the beginning of the Christian era and the end of the Middle Ages, European attitudes toward a number of minorities underwent profound transformations. Many groups passed from constituting undistinguished parts of the mainstream of society to comprising segregated, despised, and sometimes severely oppressed fringe groups. (p. 3). It was the church fathers such as Augustine and Thomas Aquinas who influenced the church on sexuality and homosexuality. They viewed any sexual acts that could not lead to conception as unnatural, and therefore sinful. Therefore, the church became powerful in regulating sexual behavior. It is no wonder there is such dysfunction within many of our churches. Back then anyone who participated in sexual behavior they did not approve of were tortured or burned at the stake. Today of course the church does not use such primitive measures. They simply will damn you to hell and make you feel guilt, shame and hate, which brings about a high rate of suicide. It is the oppression against gays and lesbians that is bringing about a high rate of suicide. Can you imagine Christians behaving in such a manner, which Jesus Himself would not approve? Here the church is supposed to be sharing God's love and forgiveness, yet they continue to play God and damn people instead. The Radical Fundamentalist Christian churches continue to spread lies as to homosexuals being the cause of AIDS, sexual abuse of children and the moral decay of America. Yet when we look at the facts, AIDS is growing among women and children. Fact is, AIDS is greatest among heterosexuals around the world. Most of all AIDS does not care who you are. AIDS is affecting us all. We can no longer blame any certain group. Second of all, the facts show that overwhelmingly their parents, grandparents or married family member sexually abuses children. Just read the paper or see the news and some parent has sexually abused their child. Lastly, those parents who drown their children in a sinking car, throw their children out in the streets to fend for themselves, and kill their child because they will not quit crying are the moral decay of America. The abominations of this country are not the homosexuals, but those heterosexuals who will not take responsibility for raising their children. Sorry for being dogmatic on the subject, but radicals see it no other way. Again we must stop blaming any certain group and realize we all have a responsibility for loving God and our neighbor as ourselves. That is what the Bible calls good morality. Boy, has the Christian

Church failed in this area. We must begin to talk about equality, fairness and dignity of all God's children. It is scary to think that anyone would want to burn homosexuals at the stake as the Christians of old did, but it could happen. PFLAG is an organization that opens its doors to parents, families and friends of gays and lesbians. They make the following statement:

> Perhaps a "culture" unto themselves are the right wing (typically Christians) fundamentalists. Most have an opinionated, unkind, hostile and unapproachable stance on homosexuality that leaves little room for change. It has been this group who has made the term sexual preference popular, that the thought being that if you can see homosexuality as a choice, then you can blame those who make this decision of how to live their lives. My son once said to me, "If it was a choice, few people would choose it since it is brought with so many difficulties." My experience is that fundamentalist parents who come to PFLAG meetings find themselves in a real bind. Often, their churches make them feel guilty and at fault for having a gay child. At a time when parents need the love and support of the church the most, many find they are ostracized (p. 164 *Gays & Lesbian Mental Health*).

So you can imagine what would happen to a homosexual who came out to his/her church and announced that they are homosexual and in a relationship with someone of the same sex. Fact is, many are asked to leave the church and never come back again. Many religious parents, upon learning their child is gay, will seek to change them through the help of clergy, psychiatrists or groups that offer a remedy for change. Many young people who have not made the change are forced into counseling, and if no changes occur are kicked out of the home. Many gays and lesbians seek change and may even say they are changed in order not to feel such oppression. Some go on into marriage to show they have changed, but in the end such marriages end up in divorce and a family that should have never been. The tragedy is that most homosexuals who seek change are unsuccessful, and attempt to, or successfully commit suicide. Many gays and lesbians come out of some sort of religious group. They, like many, are seeking a religious experience. This experience is shattered when they come out of the closet.

> Gays and lesbians often experience a sense of crisis as they begin their spiritual journeys. Because they have been labeled immature, unnatural, sick and illegal by the major institutions, and with these factors compounded by the AIDS crisis, they have difficulty appreciating the fundamental goodness of creation and the giftedness of homosexuality. The dualistic influences of their religious heritage and societal intolerance lead many to reject their bodies and feelings. What they deny and reject, they project outward on others. This is the basis for homophobia. Those who have a fear and revulsion of their own homosexual capacity tend to perceive in others what they despise and have often repressed in themselves. The fundamental spiritual challenge for gays and lesbians is to appreciate and celebrate the basic goodness of all creation, including their sexuality, without becoming possessive and addictive. (p. 103, *Is the Homosexual My Neighbor*).

We are all spiritual beings on a journey. When this journey is interrupted it can be very damaging. Many gays and lesbians who leave the church never open the doors of a church again. Those who do go back to church do so with a lot of hard work and yet still have a hard time adjusting. It is only over time that many gay and lesbian Christians find healing from the scars caused by the church of their childhood. This in itself is sad. Until the early seventies there were no churches open to homosexuals. Today, this situation has begun to make some progress in the right direction as some churches open their hearts to gays and lesbians with God's grace. Churches are beginning to see they were wrong and are correcting their misconceptions regarding homosexuals. Even with these small changes there are a lot of scars in need of healing. The psychological, mental, social and spiritual well being of gays and lesbians are damaged greatly by the radical Christian groups.

In many fundamentalist churches there are many closeted homosexuals or those seeking to change their orientation. Today, the fundamentalists have taken a new view, that homosexuality is an illness like alcoholism. These types of misconceptions causes many homosexuals to live double lives, or be something they are not. Many fundamental Christians struggling with homosexuality go through life thinking they suffer from an illness. Therefore, they live a lonely life.

> If the church takes seriously its responsibility to share Christ's love with all people, Christians must reach out to homosexual people as well as heterosexual people. That will mean not only giving serious attention to the findings of the social and behavioral sciences, but also facing up to a number of specific issues relating to the topic of homosexuality. First, we must deal with homophobia—the term coined by psychotherapist, George Weinberg, for the fear, anxiety, revulsion, and anger the subject tends to generate. Second, we need to develop an understanding of gay people as a people or community. And third, we must ask ourselves if there needs to be a rethinking of homosexuality from a Biblical and theological perspective. (p. 103, *Is the Homosexual My Neighbor*).

The good news is that churches are beginning to look more closely at the issue. Thank God for those churches that have accepted homosexuals as they are. Even with these churches, many homosexuals do not see going to church as a need in their lives. They develop their own understanding of spirituality or have no room for God. Again, the damage has been done. It will take time to bring about healing. The radical Christian groups need to gain a better understanding of sexuality in light of Biblical criticism. Dr. Nelson states it best:

Sexual questions have an inevitable religious dimension. The Christian heritage contains not only a plethora of teachings concerning sexual morality, it also bears great theological themes of sexual relevance. What we believe about creation and God's purpose in creating us as sexual beings, what we believe about human nature and destiny, what we believe about sin and salvation, about love, justice, and community—all these and many other basic beliefs will condition and shape our sexual self-understandings.

In looking at Christian tradition we have seen the downfall of sexuality in their misunderstanding of homosexuals. As we look at sexuality we can see it involves more than sex, which is a biologically-based need, which is more than procreation but, indeed, toward pleasure and tension release. Sexuality is a much more comprehensive term associated with more diffuse and symbolic meanings, psychological and cultural orientations. While sexuality includes sex, it goes beyond this point. Sexuality goes further than our thoughts and actions. It is our self-understanding and way of being in the world as male and female. As we study the human being, we realize how complicated God has made us. But in our continued search for answers we find something new about the who, what, where and why of our existence. Without this cycle we cease to grow and the world stops for that moment. The radical Christian groups are missing some of the greatest moments in life in not truly understanding the homosexual community. The loss is felt at both ends of the spectrum. In understanding more about sexuality, we experience the emotional, cognitive, physical and spiritual need for intimate communion with humanity and God. Once this cycle is broken we have altered what God intended. In conclusion, we can see how the ignorance of homosexuality within the radical Christian movement is damaging not only to the homosexual, but also to their families and friends. We can no longer live by our ignorance and stupidity about any given subject. What we don't understand comes through education. The key to homosexuality is continued education, which has only been a subject matter over the past twenty years. We are now just learning more about homosexuality on all levels. If we are dogmatic about the issue, we know very little about homosexuality and heterosexuality. But, what we are learning is important.

> Sexuality is a sign, a symbol, and a means of our call to communication and communion. This is most apparent in regard to other human beings, other body-selves. The mystery of our sexuality is the mystery of our need to reach out to embrace others both physically and spiritually. Sexuality thus expressed God's intention that we find our authentic humanness in relationship. But such humanizing relationship cannot occur on the human dimension alone. Sexuality, we must also say, is intrinsic to our relationship with God. (p. 18, *Embodiment*).

We can see the importance of homosexuality and religion. Their harmony is important to the cycle of life. God has put us all here to work in harmony with one another. It is a life long endeavor that we have not achieved. We must learn from our past regarding Jews, women and blacks. It has been religion which harbored feelings against such groups. Hopefully, we would learn from our past mistakes about certain groups. Closing thought: WE ARE ALL GOD'S CHILDREN—HIS LOVE AND GRACE EXTEND TO ALL HIS CREATION.

Chapter 2

Misconceptions Coming out of The Fundamentalist Movement Regarding Homosexuality

In this chapter, we will look at the misconceptions coming out of the radical fundamentalist groups regarding homosexuality. We will not deal with the misinterpretations of Scripture regarding homosexuality. This chapter seeks to show the radical fundamentalist understanding of homosexuality lies in ignorance and stupidity. The basis of their argument goes back to the Bible. Those so called professionals in the medical and psychological fields who stand against homosexuality base much of their conclusions upon the Bible. This is nothing new. History is full of the radical fundamentalists using the Bible against such groups as Jews, blacks, women and homosexuals. Their attitudes have caused psychological, emotional, mental and spiritual damage to such groups as just mentioned. Some people spend a lifetime dealing with the misconceptions brought against them. On the other hand, many find the truth and healing in their life. This chapter will answer the radical fundamentalist viewpoints regarding homosexuality. Secondly, will give hope to the homosexuality community. Third, will bring about healing. We can no longer live in ignorance about such issues. With our technological society, we do not have to live in fear about a particular group. This chapter will seek to educate those who are willing to learn. We realize there are those who will never see truth or educate themselves beyond their own ignorance or stupidity.

HOMOSEXUALITY IS A MENTAL DISORDER—This continues to be a message coming out of the radical fundamentalist movement. They conclude that homosexuality is a sickness. This would be understandable, if this was the 1950's or 1960's. Until the late 1960's no one had ever made objective studies of mentally healthy self-accepting homosexuals. It was assumed that none existed. For the most part, the vast majority of gays and lesbians did not openly talk about themselves. The few studies conducted back then were done on mental patients who hoped to be cured. Society, back then, looked to those who acted in the manner of a macho "dyke" or swishy "faggot" to represent the norm. Since the dark ages we know better. Thank God for the American Psychiatric and American Psychological societies who, in 1973 and 1975, declared that homosexuality is not a mental disorder.

> Until the 1970's most psychological research on homosexuality focused on its presumed pathological aspects. Morin (1977) documented the bias that dominated the field up to that time as "heterosexual bias," which he defined as "a belief system that values heterosexuality as superior to and/or more natural than homosexuality." Only a few pioneers (such as Kinsey, Pomeroy, and Martin 1948; Kinsey et al 1953; Ford and Beach, 1951; Hooker 1957) stood out as questioning the dominant model of homosexuality as a sign of mental illness. A significant change occurred as a result of a concerted effort by gay affirmative mental health professionals who called attention the empirical data that led the American Psychiatric Association in 1973 to remove homosexuality per se from its list of mental disorders. The American Psychological Association (APA) supported this change and further urged mental health professionals to take the lead in removing the stigma that previously had been associated

with homosexuality. (p. 2, *Psychological Perspectives on Lesbian and Gay Male Experience*).

There are no studies to support the mental illness of homosexuals any more than we could say that heterosexuals are mentally ill. History gives us some of the greats who changed our world. They were gay/lesbian:

1. Socrates
2. Susan B. Anthony
3. Alexander the Great
4. Hadrian
5. St. Augustine
6. Michelangelo
7. Leonardo da Vinci

8. William Shakespeare
9. Emily Dickinson
10. Eleanor Roosevelt
11. Florence Nightingale
12. Martina Navratilova
13. Elton John
14. Anna Freud (Freud's daughter)

These are just a few of the greats who were known homosexuals. To say they were mentally ill is absurd. Homosexuals are in all professions and are making a difference in this world. There are many homosexuals who go on to live healthy and happy lives. The problem is the bigotry, hatred and lies by those who seek to tear down homosexuality. This type of behavior towards any group will bring about psychological and mental anguish. Inclusion of homosexuality is a western problem.

> Inclusion of homosexuality in any international classification of disease or abnormality is problematic, and raised a number of nosologic and value related issues as well as cultural ones. It can be argued that the definition of homosexuality as abnormal is both culturally and temporally bound in western society, and thus cannot be used to describe or ascribe characteristics to individuals in other societies. (p. 247, *Male and Female Homosexuality*).

This problem stems from our strong religious beliefs, which has a hold on society. Thank God this is now taking a turn towards the best. Society is beginning to look at issues such as homosexuality with an open mind. We can no longer think of homosexuality as a handicap, sin or something unpleasant. Once we stop hating homosexuals, then we will break the cycle. Even Freud himself could not classify homosexuality as an illness.

> Freudianism does not, and more importantly, cannot see homosexuals as diseased, or as ill, or as any such thing. (That is, it does not and cannot see homosexuals as sick because of their homosexuality per se—they might be sick for other reasons). Remember that Freud himself at one point said, "homosexuality cannot be classified as an illness." (Jones 1955: 3, 208). (p. 222, *Homosexuality*).

Freud conscientiously avoided the attempt to develop any master theory to explain homosexuality. His followers used his theory of stages in psychosexual development to explain homosexuality. Their explanations led to confusion. Homosexuality has been around since recorded history. The study of homosexuality has been in medical writings and considered a fact of life. In the Christian realm it was considered a sin. It was not until the eighteenth century that there was a growing concern of sickness aspects of sexuality.

Reasons for this concern were in part due to the confusion of the effects of venereal disease with sexual activity itself. (p. 21, *Male and Female Homosexuality*).

The radical Christian movement still lives in the past regarding sexuality on any given level. Thank God for sexologists—many people no longer look upon homosexual activity as a moral lapse and as a vile sin. The sickness model has not shown any medical stability to their argument. Many homosexuals do not show any instability any more than a heterosexual does. Therefore, virtually every respectable mental health professional has rejected the claim that as a rule, gay people are less mentally stable than others.

Clearly, behind this selective focus on the "unnatural sin" of homosexuality lie deep-seated fears and anxieties—fears that have recently come to be subsumed under the concept of homophobia. Homophobia in its most intense forms represents a pathological fear of homosexuality, usually based on one or more of the following factors: (1) a deep-seated insecurity concerning one's own sexuality and gender identity, (2) a strong religious indoctrination, or (3) simple ignorance about homosexuals. (p. 19 *Homosexual Behavior A Modern Reappraisal*).

HOMOSEXUALS ARE PEDOPHILES—This is one of the big misconceptions coming out of the radical Christian movement. In many of their letters and books regarding homosexuality they mention pedophiles. They put out warnings to their families to keep watch over their children around homosexuals.

It is amazing that such people would go to any length to silence homosexuals. The fear, that the radical Christian movement tries to instill in its congregation, is that homosexuals seek to recruit their children. Wardell Pomeroy makes the following statement:

Much of what is described as "education" about homosexuality is composed of undisguised efforts to recruit children into the "lifestyle." *(Boys and Sex*, 1981).

Such stupidity has no merit. The education factor is about people knowing the facts regarding homosexuality. History has shown us that education regarding any minority group brings about freedom from bigotry and hatred. How any educated person could think that gay people recruit because they can't reproduce is absurd. Many gays and lesbians have children through various means, including adoption. Also, their children grow up to be no more gay than children of heterosexual parents.

UCLA psychiatrist Martha Kirkpatrick studied the children of single lesbian and single heterosexual mothers. She could find no difference between the two groups of children, either in terms of emotional disturbances or sexual identity. Similar results come from a recent study by Richard Green, a psychiatrist at the State University of New York at Stony Brook; Green evaluated 37 children being reared either by female homosexuals or by parents who had undergone a sexchange operation. And all of the teenagers in this group were decidedly "straight" in their sexual orientation. (p. 302, *Psychology the Science of Behavior*).

The concern noted earlier regarding homosexuals and children (family) by the radical Christian movement is based upon their bigotry and hatred. To take the issue even farther, the radical Christian movement says that homosexuals seek to molest children. The seduction by homosexuals will affect the children's sexual orientation. Once again the material suggests this is not true.

In their 1981 study, Alan Bell and his colleagues compared 1,000 homosexuals with a carefully matched group of 500 heterosexual men and women. These scientists report that the majority of both groups "know" their sexual orientation at a very early age, several years before they actually engaged in any overt sexual acts. A great many of heterosexuals had homosexual encounters at an early age, but become "straight" anyhow. And most of the homosexuals had a number of heterosexual encounters in life. They didn't find these experiences "traumatic", just less rewarding than same-sex relationships. (p. 302, *Psychology the Science of Behavior*).

Secondly, gay people are by nature predatory child molesters. This misconceived idea comes out of hate and bigotry. Once again, the facts show that pedophiles are predominately heterosexual. The Children's Hospital in Denver, Colorado, found that between July 1, 1991 and June 1992, only one of 387 cases of suspected child molestation involved a gay perpetrator. Overwhelmingly, the study found that boys and girls alike said they were abused by heterosexual male family members, including fathers, stepfathers, grandfathers and uncles. Men who molest boys are, by a wide margin, heterosexuals in any adult sexual involvement they may have. Also, many homosexuals work with children. For example many are teachers.

> It has been estimated that six thousand to ten thousand gays teach New York City school children, yet between 1930 and 1970 there was only one case of homosexual molestation. During the same period, however, many teachers were accused of improper involvement with a student of the opposite sex. (p. 101, *Now That I Know*).

The facts given show that recruitment/child molestation by homosexuals is a myth. There is no way an educated or sensible person could adhere to the radical Christian stance. Their belief has caused much damage to homosexuals on many levels. The fact is, it's hard for them to adopt children. If they have their own, they cover up their sexuality or their ex-wife or ex-husband fight for custody of the children. This causes psychological and mental anguish for many homosexuals and their children.

HOMOSEXUALITY STEMS FROM HAVING A POOR FATHER RELATIONSHIP AND A DOMINEERING MOTHER—This view came to be known shortly after the turn of the century by Freud. He observed that men with weak or absent fathers and thwarted mothers are apt to become homosexuals. The problem with this theory is that it abounds in the histories of countless heterosexual individuals. It was a psychoanalyst by the name of Bieber who conducted a study in 1962, which compounded this issue. The following personal story brings the issue close to home: While applying for a position as a substitute teacher, I needed a reference from a Baptist school at which I taught. The Baptist minister made the following statement to a question on the reference: "No gay person should teach children."

The minister's reaction is not surprising. Radical Christian churches are noted to think homosexuals seek to teach and recruit children into homosexuality. Therefore they warn their parishioners of homosexuals seeking to molest their children into the lifestyle. This chapter has sought to show the fallacies of such ignorance and stupidity. This myth is simply that, a myth. There is no truth to such thinking. For example, this chapter can begin to answer such actions as the Baptist minister. We can no longer allow such misinformation to be allocated without counter-attacking such beliefs. This chapter has simply done just that.

Also, Dr. Bell, Weinberg, and Hammersmith, in their 1981 book titled "Sexual Preference," saw no support for Beiber's conclusions. Also, their study is the most extensive work done today.

Clinical evidence, however, demonstrates that this general-ization does not always hold true. Over the years I have seen a number of homosexuals who had close relationships with affectionate and caring fathers. Evans and Siegelman report similar findings. Moreover, if the strong-mother/weak-or absent-father constellation were a determining factor, one would expect to find a much higher incidence of male homo-sexuality among urban blacks, since life in the black ghetto has for decades, produced a large number of broken homes in which the mother was the mainstay of family life. However, there is no evidence that the incidence of homosexuality is any greater in black men than in white men. (p. 11, *Homosexual Behavior a Modern Re-appraisal*).

Show us a homosexual, who comes from a dysfunctional family and we will show you a heterosexual who comes from a dysfunctional family. We cannot blame one's sexuality on any aspect of the family system. This theory does not have any support.

Overtly, the old psychoanalytic bugaboos are dead: there is no evidence, according to the Kinsey Institute, that male homosexuality is caused by dominant mothers and/or weak fathers, or that female homosexuality is caused by girls having exclusively male role models. (p. 141, *Human Sexuality Opposing Viewpoints*).

HOMOSEXUALS ARE THE REASON FOR AIDS—This is another bigotry remark made by the radical Christian movement. They go on to say it's God's judgment against homosexuals. This is the ultimate in stupidity. There is nothing to support their allegations. "About 75 percent of people with AIDS throughout the world are heterosexual." (*How You Can Avoid Getting AIDS* by Earvin "Magic" Johnson). AIDS was high at first in the homosexual community, but that has changed. It has gone down in the homosexual community. In the last few years it has grown in the heterosexual community in America. But worldwide, it has always been big in the heterosexual community. There should be no blame. It is all of our problem. AIDS is not concerned with orientation, status, color, and religion. AIDS affects us all. The professionals do not accept the notion that AIDS is a gay disease.

The disease now called AIDS or advanced HIV disease was first recognized about 10 years ago. Although many of the early AIDS patients were gay (homosexual) men—that is, men who have sex with other men—and most persons with AIDS in the United States are gay men, many persons who are not gay are infected with HIV and their numbers are increasing. Because there are many ways of contracting HIV, the fact that a man is infected with HIV or has symptoms of advanced HIV disease does NOT mean he is a homosexual. A man does not have to have sexual relations with another man to contract the HIV disease. Many men and women and their babies have become infected with HIV as a result of using intravenous drugs, receiving blood transfusions, or blood products, or through heterosexual (straight) relations that is, sex between a man and a woman. (p. 5, *Important Information For All People About HIV/AIDS: An Update*).

Today, HIV is growing among women and children at an alarming rate. It is going down in the homosexual community, but growing in the heterosexual community at a great rate. We need to realize that AIDS is all our problem. Let us come together to find a cure, and stop blaming any particular group.

In closing, these are just a few issues that the radical Christian movement would have you believe about homosexuality. Their history is full of their bigotry and hatred. They use the Bible as their foundation. In the name of God they sought to tear down blacks, women, Jews, and now homosexuals. More than any other book; the Bible has shaped Western Civilization's opinion of homosexuality by their misinterpretation of several Biblical passages they give excuse to murder, torture, imprisonment, rape, battery, ostracize, deride and discrimination against gays and lesbians. Ask a black person who lived during slavery how they felt about themselves? How many of them killed themselves, due to the bigotry and hatred towards them? How many of them suffered psychological and mental anguish? Time heals all wounds. But, even today, black people feel the hurts of the past. We cannot expect less from the homosexual community. The radical Christian movement would have us believe homosexuals are mentally disturbed. The issue is survival. Just like the black people in slavery and the Jews in the Holocaust. Homosexuals have learned to survive just like blacks and Jews. What we have are heroes who have overcome great odds.

Yet primarily on the basis of these religious teachings, homosexuals have been subjected to legal discrimination and persecution throughout Western culture for almost two millennia, at times in proportions bordering on genocide. As Crompton (1978), has pointed out, homosexuals were extensively brutalized and murdered, first by the ancient Hebrews around 550 BC and then about 850 years later when

Christianity came into power in Western Europe. Genocide laws against homosexuals remained in the criminal codes in France until 1791, in England until 1861, and in Scotland, as late as 1889. Both male and female homosexuals were subject to capital punishment in a number of the American colonies, but the death penalty was gradually revoked after the revolution. The most recent episode of genocide of homosexuals was in Hitler's Germany when more that 50,000 of them in Germany alone were arrested and sent to perish in concentration camps. When those seized by the Nazis in occupied countries are added, estimates of the number of homosexuals who died from illness, neglect, medical experimentation, and the gas chamber, range from 100,000 to more than 400,000 (Crompton, 1978). (p. 19, *Homosexual Behavior A Modern Reappraisal*).

Our history has a lot of bigotry and hatred. We should learn from our mistakes. It causes a lot of physical, psychological, emotional, and spiritual pain in people. The pain can have lasting results.

Hanley-Hackenbruck (1989) suggests that therapeutic exploration of low self-esteem in gay men and lesbians will uncover internalized homophobia, which has served to cause the individual "severe anxiety, depression, sexual dysfunction, relationship failures, or a feeling of being an impostor" (p. 35). Resolution of internalized homophobia (or "superego modification," as she terms it) is an in-depth process that includes further individuating the person from parental domination (and family perspectives and values concerning homosexuality), defining one's own values and thus defining a sexual identity, and developing an oftentimes new social and peer group that is more accepting of the person. Only in recent years has there been adequate attention given to gay male self-esteem and the self-image gay men maintain of themselves (Voeller, 1980; Cornett, 1993). Clearly, growing up in American society where homosexuality is so ridiculed, condemned, and stereotyped creates an internal struggle for a healthy sense of self. Without sufficient internal and external validation of worth, developing the self-confidence and assuredness that comprises much of self-esteem can be difficult to attain. This carries with it inherent risks for achieving healthy individuation and identity. (p. 1-2, *Gay & Lesbian Mental Health*).

The good thing is that many homosexuals overcome their situations. Once they realize who they are as a person—that being homosexual is not something bad or a sin. Overcoming such bigotry and hatred takes time. So, to all those who have overcome some type of bigotry: good job!

Chapter 3

The Condemnation Dilemma

It is sad when a religious group of any kind seeks to condemn any person or group. Our book focuses upon those Christian churches who have had their share of condemning minority groups. The message of the Bible is God's love and forgiveness:

> For God so loved the world that He gave His only begotten Son, that whosoever believes in Him will not perish, but have everlasting life. For God did not send the Son into the world to judge the world, but that the world should be saved through Him. (John 3:16-17 *New American Standard Bible*).

This is the very foundation of the Christian faith. When a certain segment of the Christian church seeks to condemn homosexuals we must address this issue. Maybe you have felt the wrath of the radical Christian churches, which led you away from God. On the other hand, maybe you are one who has condemned homosexuals. We need to realize what damage is done when we condemn anyone. In this situation, many gays and lesbians feel the wrath of God, which causes psychological and spiritual ramifications. There are many gays and lesbians who want to worship the God they grew up with, but cannot, because of the condemnation they will feel for being open about their homosexuality. Today there is a fundamentalist group of gay

Christians who are a part of an affiliation called The Atlantic Association of Christian Churches. Their message is that Christ died for them and by faith take the gift of Eternal Life. They embrace their homosexuality and do not see it as a sin – but that gays and lesbians are wonderfully made in the eyes of God. Unfortunately, not every Christian who might be struggling with their orientation and faith finds their way into The Atlantic Association of Christian Churches. Therefore, they leave the church believing that God hates them for being gay or lesbian. Maybe you are there. Those who are not gay or lesbian, can you imagine the pain and hurt such people must go through because a certain aspect of the Christian churches chose to condemn? Those coming out of the radical Christian churches by choice or force, are like the Israelites wondering in the wilderness. They are a people without a home. Any type of condemnation towards any group such as the Jews felt during the Holocaust, has lasting results. Many end up with emotional scars, which psychotherapy helps in addressing the origin of these narcissistic injuries. Religion, when given properly, releases a sense of something greater than self, as sense of community, answers to life questions and guidance. On the other hand when religion becomes condemning, it can be extremely painful. A professional psychotherapist puts it this way:

> When these needs are not met for lesbians and gay men, because of homophobia, a special set of betrayals and conflicts develops. In response, some choose to hide within the mainstream of their church, not letting anyone know that they are gay, some decide to fight homophobia overtly, some join alternative sects within, and some create new forms for worship and spirituality. These struggles, decisions, and questions are sometimes a central part of someone's psychotherapy. (p. 175, *Gay & Lesbian Mental Health*).

Some never go back to church, because of the pain caused. The issue goes even further than church. Those gays and lesbians who never dawn a church usually carry a lot of anger towards God. They can also suffer from low self-esteem, guilt and depression. Now we can see what can happen to a person who is condemned based on their sexual orientation (Homosexuality). This is just the psychological, mental and spiritual damage done. Throughout this book we will interchange the words bigotry and hatred with homophobia. Those who express their bigotry and hatred towards homosexuals do so out of ignorance and stupidity. Those from the radical Christian churches usually follow the teachings of their leader. They never take into consideration what the Bible really has to say on the subject of homosexuality. More important, they fail to see the damage caused by their condemnation towards gays and lesbians. It has lasting results against the person, their family and friends. Those who overcome the bigotry and hatred are survivors. Overcoming comes with a price for many gays and lesbians. They are condemned by their church, families and friends. It is not surprising that some gays and lesbians try to conform.

> With the bombardment of negative messages telling us what gay people are supposed to be like, the resulting injuries to self-esteem, and the energy that goes into hiding true feelings, it is small wonder that most gay people yield to the massive pressures and try to conform to the popular image of the "normal" person. The first effort to conform usually goes on for years. More often than not, the gay person is aware of gay feelings long before he considers himself or herself eligible for the label. Much effort goes into explaining to oneself why the feelings are there. The attempts at explanation are usually extracted from the antigay myths of our culture. I may decide that gay feelings are stemming from having a strong mother and a weak father, or an absent mother and a disagreeable father, or any other psychoanalytic caricature of my true family situation. Or I may believe that the feelings come from having been infected by evil and that Satan has a grip on me. Or I might believe it is an inherited defect, just like Uncle Charles or Aunt Ruth, who were put away or committed suicide. Or I

may believe that I am losing my mind because I have been bat-
tling the issue. Or I may simply believe that I have been hang-
ing out with the wrong crowd. Whatever the presumed
genesis of the feelings, the next effort in the struggle to conform is to guard against these gay feelings being translated
into behavior. (p. 32, 33, *Loving Someone Gay*).

Can you imagine being something you are not? Suppressing your
true feelings, because of anti-gay myths coming from a certain group?
This type of confusion can cause havoc on a person's well being. In
reality it does. It also takes years of counseling for such gays who struggled to conform to something they are not. Those who do come to grips
with who they are as a gay person, do so with a price. Here are some of
the statements coming out of the radical Christian movement, which
causes scars for gays, lesbians, their family and friends. These statements are not what God intends. Also not every church supports these
statements. The fact that they are being made is all we need to know:

It was a hot summer day in Miami, Florida and Pedro Zamora
had died from complications from AIDS. Over 1,500 gather for
a memorial in honor of his life. In the midst of this gathering
was a Baptist minister by the name of Fred Phelps and his followers who were holding signs that read "God hates fags",
"Fag Funeral", "Pedro in Hell", 2 Gay rights: AIDS & Hell."
This is the extreme of the radical religious message. You might
even say this man was sick, which no doubt he is. This is why
messages of bigotry, hatred and lies about gays and lesbians in
the hands of some jealous religious freak can be deadly. Fred
Phelps is just one of those religious leaders who make such
sick statements towards gays and lesbians. He even wrote
about me in headlines saying: "Fag Baptist preacher wants to
debate Phelps (Fags are masochists)." The fax he sent me had
my partner and I with 666 written on our foreheads. You say
how sick and unchristian. You're right; it is about the sickness
of hate and bitterness and such behavior, that this book is

being written. It is time to stop the hate, bigotry, and lies about gays and lesbians.

Can you believe that such loving Christians would make such statements. It is amazing that they preach love on one hand and hate on the other. Such statements have lasting results upon a person's psychological well being. The radical Christian's misconceptions about homosexuals lead to the oppression of gays and lesbians. It forces them to stay in the closet, which is psychological and mental torture.

> While gay men and lesbians have been consistently involved in the institutional forms of Judeo-Christianity through history, those institutions have themselves failed to accept or support openly gay individual couples, either professionally, liturgically/pastorally, or doctrinally. Judeo-Christianity has, instead, encouraged homophobia in society, thereby fostering antigay oppression, which dehumanizes gay individuals, undermines gay couplings, and exacerbates familiar tensions between gay and non-gay relatives. (p. 265, *Homosexuality and Family Relations*).

It is not surprising, that many gays and lesbians end up in counseling. No human should have to go through such oppression. Even the Bible spoke against such actions. The Bible uses other words such as to bruise, to put down, to distress and crush. These are, no doubt, strong words with lasting results. In God's eyes, such oppression is a gross evil. God always took the side of the oppressed. At the interpersonal level, agape—love is the primary norm of action against oppression. Yet, we fail to see this love in the radical Christian churches who condemn homosexuals at any cost. In the name of God some people seek to bring condemnation against anything or anyone they do not agree with. This type of thinking leads to unneeded guilt and shame.

> Guilt is at the basis of much human suffering. "I'll never get used to it," one counselor has said, "There is no box big

enough to hold all the persons with guilt. They are all unique
and need to be seen as individuals." (p. 135, *Christian
Counseling*).

The radical Christian churches cause unwanted guilt, which brings
about mental anguish to the homosexual community. Then it takes a
counselor years to help alleviate such pain. Sometimes the pain never
goes completely away. The issues begin at birth. Our development of
social and sexual identity begins at birth and continues until we die.
The problem in the past has been the idea that children grow up to be
heterosexuals. The past has given very little acknowledgment that
some children are homosexual. Today's gays and lesbians have a past
history to contend with. Our gay youth have their peers to follow. That
does not give them much to follow. But society is making some positive moves regarding gays and lesbians. We have begun to answer the
myths coming out of the radical Christian churches regarding homosexuality. It is the truths about gays and lesbians, which will set the
homosexual free from the oppression. The problem begins when they
suppress who they are as a homosexual. The radical Christian church
does not help the situation when they seek to condemn gays and lesbians. They place blame, guilt, and shame upon such persons and
their families. What comes out of it is silence.

Lesbian or gay youth are often also afraid to share their feelings with people they are attracted to because they know they
may be rebuffed publicly, ridiculed, scorned, or rejected. A
variety of problems can arise from these and other negative
interactions. Problems can range from poor self-esteem to
poor school attendance or performance, substance abuse, par-
ticipation in prostitution and pornography (both male and
female) suicidal ideation or attempts, and running away from
or leaving home. (p. 149-150, *The Counseling Source Boo*k).

The closet is the worst place for gays and lesbians. Many adult gays
never find themselves until their adulthood. Therefore, they experience

a part of their childhood in adulthood. One of the big problems that comes out of this whole mess is the damaged self-esteem.

> Self-esteem is the elusive but essential ingredient of every healthy personality. Our sense of self-worth determines how well we function in every area of our lives, from our feelings to our behavior to our careers to our relationships with others to our relationship with God. Our self-esteem shapes our attitude toward life and determines whether we face the challenges of life with a "yes I can" or "no I can't" attitude. Our self-esteem is either the launching pad of our successes or the trap that triggers our failures. (p. 494-495, *The Complete Life Encyclopedia*).

The only good thing that comes out of damaged self-esteem is when one knows the source, such as the radical Christian churches condemnation, bigotry and hatred toward gays and lesbians. In understanding the source one can make a step towards becoming emotionally whole and healthy. The steps are slow and pains taking. Breaking the silence is just the beginning to psychological and spiritual wholeness. The rest of the battle will take a lot of energy and survival tactics to win the battle over homophobia. This battle does not just affect gays and lesbians, but all those around them. As the gay and lesbian begins to grow stronger in self-esteem, they are able to go on living a productive life. Their growth may be with or without their families and friends. Unfortunately, some of the family and friends are a part of the radical Christian churches. What is alarming with the radical Christian churches is their strong belief of family. Yet they feel no sense of loss to forsake their children, parents or friends on the basis of their orientation. Something is not right with this picture. It truly is a contradiction in the making. Each gay and lesbian comes from a family. They should not have to choose between their orientation and family. If you are confused, so are we. Bigotry on any level does not make any sense, especially those who preach love and family. We know that many gays and lesbians have their own families. Also, many have strong ties with their parents and siblings. So, we can see the effects of the radical Christian churches have not affected all people. For those gays and lesbians who have been affected but overcome, we salute them. The healing process is not easy. Damage to the psychological and mental wellbeing of a person happens over time, therefore, the recovery time is just as long. We can see that the condemnation of homosexuals by the radical Christian churches has a domino effect, which leads to a combination of ills, such as low self-esteem, guilt, shame, hate and even death. The message from the radical Christian group towards homosexuality must be stopped. The psychological roller coaster is affecting many people. It not only affects the homosexual, but their family and friends. Freud himself wrote a letter to a mother of a gay son:

Homosexuality is assuredly no advantage but it is nothing to be ashamed of, no vice, no degradation, it cannot be classified as an illness. Many highly respected individuals of ancient and modern times have been homosexuals, several of the great men among them Plato, Michelangelo, Leonardo da Vinci, etc. It is a great injustice to persecute homosexuality as a crime and cruelty, too. (Masters, Johns, Kolodny).

The radical Christian movement seeks to use the Bible as their guide to explain away homosexuality. Not only do we find fault in their interpretation of Scripture, but also a contradiction. For example, John 3:16-17 totally contradicts the word condemnation. It points to God's love, not judgment. Why, then, do the radical Christians seek to condemn/judge homosexuals? This is a question that needs to be answered. There is no single answer. Some of the problems are based on ignorance, stupidity and hatred. The hostility and fear most people have towards gays and lesbians is called Homophobia. If you speak with a radical Christian, they will say they are not Homophobic. Yet, it has been their message of homosexuality being a sin, sick, unnatural, contagious and depraved that screams Homophobic.

Clearly, behind this selective focus on the "unnatural sin" of homosexuality, lie deep-seated fears and anxieties—fears that have recently come to be subsumed under the concept of homophobia. Homophobia, in its most intense form, represents a pathological fear

of homosexuality, usually based on one or more of the following factors: (1) a deep-seated insecurity concerning one's own sexuality and
gender identity, (2) a strong religious indoctrination, or (3) simple
ignorance about homosexuals. (p. 19, *Homosexual Behavior A Modern
Re-appraisal*).

It is the message of sin, sick, unnatural, contagious and depraved
that causes problems. The message could not be further from the truth.
They go to the Bible as their proof. It is their misuse of Scriptures that
becomes the evidence against homosexuality. In the last few years the
radical Christians have sought to give not only a Biblical account, but
also a scientific account against homosexuality. They rest heavily upon
the unloving father and dominating mother complex. It is this complex which causes homosexuality. This misguided theory has not
proof or evidence to its concept. Both the American Psychological and
Psychiatric Association have stated there is no evidence to support
such a claim. In scientific terms it would be an identity problem.
Again, the America Psychiatric Association rejects Gender Identity
Disorder as a diagnosis saying that such an understanding is harmful
and implies people have a disease. Not only does it hurt gays and lesbians, but also the parents. Such an understanding says someone did
something wrong to become who they are. Of course the radical
Christians will cry out that homosexuality is unnatural. In Dr. Judd
Marmor's book *Homosexual Behavior A Modern Reappraisal he* shows a
natural perspective to homosexuality. Many other studies show a
genetic link to homosexuality. Such studies conducted by Dr. Baily, Dr.
LeVay, Dr. Reite, Dr. Allen, Dr. Gorski and the National Cancer
Institute show a genetic link to homosexuality. Yet the radical
Christians seem to ignore these facts. They continue to preach their
stupidity and ignorance. In the long run their tactics cause damage to
gays and lesbians. Their hate, bigotry and lies keep gays and lesbians
in the closet. It fuels hate from society. The damage is caused to gays
and lesbians alone. This does not include society as a whole in regards
to acceptance of homosexuality. It is oppression that brings about hurt,
low self-esteem, fear, hate and the list goes on. The issue is not about

acceptance of oneself, but how society as a whole fuels this issue. Coming out of the closet for gays and lesbians is not easy. It is a long process and sometimes takes a lifetime to reach. That's how far the radical Christians have aided in the outcome of homosexuality. It is their thinking that has caused an oppressed people to stay that way. Hopefully books like this will begin to lift this oppression and bring about healing.

Chapter 4

What does God Say?

This is the big question. In this book we have dealt with gays and lesbians, but the real focus has been with gay Christians. Knowing what God says on the subject of homosexuality is important to gay Christians. More important is the effect the radical Christian movement has had upon society regarding gays and lesbians. Most of society does not realize this affect. Therefore, answering the Bible questions regarding homosexuality is important to the well being of the gay Christian. It is noted that many gay Christians think or follow through with suicide. When gays and lesbians are told they are going to hell for being a homosexual they try to change. When they realize they cannot change they feel guilty and ashamed. When all fails for them to change their feelings, they contemplate suicide, which some follow through with. In this chapter we will look at what the Scriptures say on the subject of homosexuality. We cannot begin to look at the Scriptures until we understand the principles for Biblical interpretation. Just like there are principles for understanding reading, writing, and arithmetic, it is no different with the Bible. We know for example that $1 + 1 = 2$, because the principles for addition allot for the proper answer. It is no different in understanding the Bible. Unfortunately, many Christians do not even know the principles for Biblical Hermeneutics. It is not surprising that many

Christians would misinterpret Scriptures to condemn homosexuals. As we noted in other chapters, that the radical Christian movement history is full of bigotry and hatred towards minority groups. The basis of their bigotry was backed up by Scripture. Therefore, the following principles are very important in properly interpreting Scriptures:

1. THE LITERAL PRINCIPLE—While there is figurative symbolism and allegory, literal comes first.

2. THE HISTORICAL PRINCIPLE—This is the study of the historical setting of the Bible.

3. THE GRAMMATICAL PRINCIPLE—Terms and language of the Bible. The Bible was written in Hebrew, Greek, and Aramaic.

4. THE SYNTHESIS PRINCIPLE—That no part of the Bible contradicts any other part. We can only understand the Bible when we look at all of the Scriptures in order to understand proper theology. We cannot build theology upon part of a verse.

5. THE PRACTICAL PRINCIPLE—What does it have to do with me? In other words what is the passage saying to us today?

Without these principles we can make the Scriptures say anything we want. In the case of gays and lesbians, the radical Christian movement has used the Scriptures to bring about condemnation. We know the damage that has been caused against gays and lesbians. Such damage as low self-esteem, misguided identity, fear, guilt and shame. These are just a few of the psychological and spiritual damage caused against gays and lesbians. Many leave the church and never return. Without closure many build up anger and hate, which affect themselves and those around them. Having closure will help bring about healing. Before we look at the Scripture, we need to look at some other issues that shed light on the subject of gays and lesbians. There was a point and time in our history, when the church considered the black person to be a curse from Cain who killed Abel. At one time our "white" churches took the story in Genesis to mean the generation of black people. This ridiculous belief gave way to slavery and that black people were a lower form of mankind. It did not allow black people to learn, grow, and bloom. It suppressed and altered the psychological, social, mental and spiritual well being of God's creation. Today, we still see the results from slavery and bigotry. There are churches today that still support the thinking of the past. This is exactly the type of reasoning that has proven time and again the bigotry and ignorance of the church.

> Homosexuality is compared to a fishbone caught in the church's throat that the church can neither eject nor swallow entirely. Authors, in all denominations, have made policy statements on homosexuality. Four such stances discussed here highlight some of the common issues denominations face in their re-examination of the subject. Homosexuals struggling for full acceptance in the church must confront the classical understanding of the human being and human sexual differentiation as these concepts have traditionally influenced the churches. (p. 7, *Homosexuality and Religion*).

The view of homosexuality from the radical Christian churches has been, and still is, to change or suppress the feelings of gays and lesbians. Their message is that homosexuals have a mental illness and what they do is a sin. The radical Christian churches encourage homosexuals to seek professional psychological help in order to change the situation or at least learn to control the impulses. This type of thinking has not always been a part of society. We know that homosexuality has been around since the written page. The radical Christian churches say that God made Adam and Eve not Adam and Steve. The basis of their thinking comes from Genesis, Chapter 2, in the making of man and woman. There is no mention of gays and lesbians. This is true, but it does not take away the fact they exist and are a part of history. So where do gays and lesbians come from? This question is just as complex as understanding homosexuality and heterosexuality. There is a good theory that answers this question. In Genesis 10:1-11:26, we find the story of the Tower of Babel. It was here that God scattered the people all over the world. God also changed their language. It would only seem logical, that if God went to the trouble of changing man's surroundings and language, why not his sexual orientation? It seems that God only wanted to give diversity to mankind. This diversity has caused hatred throughout the centuries, yet God's love still abounds for all of mankind. God's love even extends to gays and lesbians. Maybe gays and lesbians are one of the diverse situations that God put into motion. The important thing about the diversity God made was for it to unite in harmony. Even at the end of time the Bible says the lamb will sit with the lion. There will be peace and harmony. The radical Christian churches have not gotten the message of harmony in the midst of diversity. We know today that one's orientation is not something anyone chooses, but a gift from God. Therefore, gays and lesbians are beginning to stand proud of their heritage, which is found in the pages of history. The issue of homosexuality was not an important issue at the beginning of Christianity.

> The Bible was not the only or even the principal source of early Christian ethics, and the Biblical passages, purportedly relating to homosexuality, had little to do with early Christian misgivings on the subject. Very few influential theologians based objections to homosexual practices on the New Testament passages now claimed to derogate such behavior, those who did, invoked them only as support for arguments based primarily on other authorities. It is, moreover, quite clear that nothing in the Bible would have categorically precluded homosexual relations among early Christians. In spite of misleading English translations that may imply the contrary, the word "homosexual" does not occur in the Bible: no extant text or manuscript, Hebrew, Greek, Syrian, or Aramaic contains such a word. (p. 92, *Christianity, Social Tolerance, and Homosexuality*).

It seems that twentieth century Christianity has sought to make homosexuality a major issue. We see this in some new translations, which insert the word homosexual in certain passages. Those who know Biblical languages know the word homosexual was not coined until the late 1800's. What we have today, is bigotry and hatred against gays and lesbians by a group who uses the Bible at their leisure. This point is seen in the theory that AIDS is God's judgement against homosexuals. We talked briefly about this in an earlier chapter. Here we will look more closely at this issue. Since the beginning of AIDS, homosexuals have taken the blame. There have been those who have said homosexuals deserve AIDS. Christians have said it's God's punishment against their perverted behavior. When someone (homosexual/heterosexual) finds out they are HIV+, they experience many emotions. There is shock, denial, anxiety, fear, anger, depression and guilt. Add to this: blaming and deserving AIDS, does not alleviate these emotions, but compounds them. Many who are found out to be HIV+, are abandoned and left to die. In this situation many have committed suicide. Even living without support and encouragement can lead to the advancement of HIV to full blown AIDS. The radical Christian view is based upon ignorance and bigotry. To say that AIDS is God's judgment against homosexuals is not seen in theology of medicine. The fact is, AIDS hits any group of people. The problem we see in this group is that of stupidity—the lack of knowledge regarding proper theology in light of history. In other words, understanding the church in sequence of Grace. Most Christians will agree we are in the Age of Grace, or as we call it, "the Dispensation of Grace." With this in mind, we can now look at this issue from a Biblical point of view. This is an important point to the gay and lesbian Christians. They have a strong belief in the Bible and its message. The key point about Scripture is its message of God's love. In the Old Testament, the people were bound by the law, but in the New Testament, Jesus came to fulfill the law. When Jesus came, lived, died, and rose from the dead it released Christians from the law. Therefore, we today, are under Grace and not bound or judged by the law. Jesus Himself, made this clear in

Matthew 5:17. Also in Romans chapter 7 and 8, Paul deals with this very issue. Paul basically is saying to the church, that we are no longer under the law, but under grace which is: God's Riches At Christ's Expense.

After all is said and done, Paul makes a beautiful statement. "There is therefore, now, no condemnation for those who are in Christ Jesus." (Romans 8:1) What a promise for those who know Jesus Christ, who is the foundation of the Christian faith. Jesus is the very core of Christianity, our only pass into heaven. We would all agree Jesus is the answer, but mention homosexual Christians and this issue changes for some. What gay Christians need to know is the Word of God does not change. As we look at the Gospel message we see Jesus' message (John 3:16-18; Romans 10:9-10; John 1:12; Hebrews 11:1; 1 John 4:15; and Revelations 3:20). In each one of these passages, Jesus is seen as our only answer. He is our way into heavenly gates. Therefore, God's main purpose is not to send judgment upon man, but to save man through Jesus Christ. It is a gift we simply must take. Those Christians who come to the realization they are gay become clouded by the condemnation and rebuke of their pastors and leaders. Those gay Christians who overcome this condemnation have been set free by the truth within these pages. The Greek word for judgement means justice, accusation, condemnation and damnation. According to its meaning, what is judgment's relationship between God and man? It is at this point that many have lost sight of its Biblical understanding in light of its historical conjunction. The basis of the New Testament is seen in John 3:16-17. In the Old Testament we saw God's judgment against many nations, but in the New Testament, God's direction takes a turn. All of the other Gospels and Epistles agree with John 3:16-17. The only judgment we see against many by God is in the future. During this dispensation of Grace, God is showing His mercy and love. His judgment will come at the end of the "Church Age." Wilmington's Guide to the Bible gives us a summary of God's judgment:

3.   Future Judgements
    a.   The (bema) judgement seat of Christ (I Cor. 3:9-15; II Cor. 5:10; Rom. 14:10; Rev. 22:12).
           1)   Upon man's religious systems (Rev. 17).
           2)   Upon man's economic and political systems (Rev. 18)
           3)   Upon man's military systems (Rev. 19: 11-21).
           4)   Upon man himself (Rev. 6, 8, 9, 16).
    c.   The lamp and talent judgment. This refers to Israel (Mt. 24:45-512; 25:1-30; Ezek. 20:33-38).
    d.   The sheep and goat judgment. This refers to the gentiles (Mt. 25:31-46).
    e.   The judgment upon the antichrist and false prophet (Rev. 19:20).
    f.   The judgment upon Satan
           1)   In the bottomless pit for one thousand years (Rev. 20:1-3).
           2)   In the lake of fire forever (Rev. 20:10).
    g.   The fallen angel judgment (I Cor. 6:3; Pet. 2:4; Jude 1:6).
    h.   The great white throne judgment (Rev. 20:11-15).

Dr. Wilmington shows us God's future judgments, which is seen after the church has been raptured. The judgment of God is seen at the beginning of the tribulation. From the conception of the church to its very end, there is no judging. It is not until the church is taken out of this present world, that judgment begins. Some try to stretch the Scriptures to say that there are present day judgments. They use such Scripture as Heb. 12:3-13; I Cor. 11:30; I Peter 4:17; John 5:16; and Acts 5:1-11 as justification. Therefore, in conclusion we can be assured that AIDS is not God's judgment against the homosexual, but another of Satan's tools to cause confusion and tear down the very essence of the Gospel of Christ. It is not who we are (homosexual/heterosexual), but what we are in Christ who will someday bring us into the glorious ages. From past history, one sees religions of all kinds placing the blame of great plagues upon God. One must remember that God allows certain things to happen that are not of His doing, but of Satan. But the church again fails to reach out to those in need. When the church does not reach out, they seem to only condemn and play God.

> The present crisis demands a radical shift in our attitudes as clergy, laity, and the church…though not exhaustive, the following are some of the things we need to do if we are to respond to the AIDS crisis in our communities as pastors and care givers:
>
> 1) We must examine our thoughts, feelings, biases, prejudices, and fears as far as AIDS and those associated with the disease are concerned. Pastoral care requires continued critical engagement of our personal values, religious beliefs, and theologies.
>
> 2) We must learn to listen—especially to those from whom we have not heard before—homosexuals, bisexuals, and intravenous drug users. We must learn to listen with the "third ear," non-judgmental, in order to understand and accept what is reality for them.
>
> 3) We must come to the realization that the acceptance of another's reality—what is real and of value to them—does not imply that we agree with that reality. Our role is not to judge or reject. We are here to show God's love by our visible presence. We must become, in essence, incarnations of the Word of God. (p. 19, *Does the Church Care?* Calvin Morris).

Dr. Morris' last point exemplifies the very problem of the church today. We have forgotten our role as messengers of God's love. We have become judges—which is God's role—not ours. Scriptures are clear as to who the judge is and who it is not (Matt. 7:1; Luke 6:37; and 12:14). The church has failed, once again, to be a place of refuge for those in need of their help. Our churches have become a courtroom instead of a haven of rest.

In the case of AIDS, we know that no one is to blame. It is a terrible disease just like cancer, which attacks many wonderful people. AIDS is not a respecter of age, sex, color, status, religion, or sexual orientation. It is a dreadful disease, which is unfortunate, but still is a part of this fallen world.

Let us pray, therefore, that a cure is found. There needs to be no more blame, shame, and guilt put on any person with AIDS.

> Guilt literally makes us sick. Guilty people become ill more than others because our ability to ward off infection is lowered from this negative emotion. For some, the guilt becomes so intense that they begin to hallucinate and see the horrors of life manifested in visions of an unreal world. For others, guilt attacks them through their nightmares, revealing to the subconscious that something is not right and must be attended to. Guilt will not be ignored. The great preacher, Charles Spurgeon said, "Beware of no man more than yourself, we carry the worst enemies within us." There is no enemy worse than guilt. It lives within us and destroys our ability to function normally in the world. When guilt is allowed to prosper, a person will not. (p. 152, *How Will I Tell My Mother?*)

We see that guilt causes many psychological, mental, physical, and spiritual problems with people who have AIDS. Let's stop the blaming, shame, and guilt. Now we turn our thoughts to the Scriptures, which form the basis of those who continue to condemn homosexuality. In giving answers to the radical Christians continued license to practice bigotry and hatred against such groups as gays and lesbians. The following story will build a foundation to why we feel this chapter is important. After seeing an ad in a college newspaper supporting Gays and Lesbians, a young man tells us the following story:

Dear people, this ad came to my mother with some other mail she received from Christian Leadership Ministries. I know she would never have replied, because she hated gay people, even me, her own (gay) son. She once said, "All gay people should get AIDS and die, just for being gay." Her outlook on homosexuality was formed early in her life. There was no way of changing her mind. My mother died on April 29, 1995 and I am sending a small donation in memory of my mother. Enclosed is a copy of her obituary. Every time someone like my mother leaves this world (dies), I feel there is one less stumbling block in the wave of equal rights for gay people. God bless all the gay people on this planet.

It is stories such as this one, that makes this chapter so important to the psychological and spiritual well being of gay Christians.

WHAT ABOUT SODOM AND GOMORRAH?

When most fundamentalists talk about homosexuals, they go back to the story of Sodom and Gomorrah. From their youth, they are told Sodom and Gomorrah was destroyed mainly because they engaged in homosexual acts. Dr. Kenneth Gangel, makes a similar statement in his book, The Gospel and The Gay, where he states, "God destroyed Sodom and Gomorrah on the basis of a particular sin: The sin was homosexuality, and the cities were Sodom and Gomorrah." In this chapter we will put this myth to rest. The fundamentalists have trans-lated the word Sodom, Sodomy and Sodomite to mean homosexual. We will also show the error of this understanding. In order to properly understand Sodom and Gomorrah, we need to go back to the very structure of interpreting the Scriptures; the principles of Hermeneutics, which consist of historical, grammatical, and literal interpretations. These three principles are the essential tools needed in order to properly understand the Scriptures. We will look at all three of these tools in detail.

It is not surprising that the Bible denies Gangel's claim in at least three places: Gen. 18:20-21, indicates that God has planned the destruction of those cities for their wickedness long before the incident at Lot's house took place. In addition, Genesis 19 is the only reference to an attempted interpretation of a homosexual act by the men of Sodom. In light of this, Gangel's sweeping accusation that "sexual recreation was rampant in the city to the point that gay crowds roamed the streets demanding sexual relations with every stranger who visited town" seems strange indeed. (p. 65, *Gays Under Grace*).

The problem with homophobic Christians, such as Dr. Gangel, is that they have a tendency to center on one incident and make an issue of it that is exaggerated beyond truth. The sins of Sodom included pride of wealth, affluence, and lack of concern for the poor as well as haughtiness, adultery and other sins (Ezekiel 16:49; Jeremiah 23:14), but the issue of homosexuality is never mentioned. In Matthew 10:14-15, Jesus Himself made no mention of homosexual condemnation in Sodom but did make a great statement about the lack of hospitality, which destroyed the two cities. Again, there were other sins rampant in the cities, but homosexuality was not one of them. Yet the radical Christian churches seek to blame the destruction of two cities upon homosexuals. To place such blame upon gays and lesbians is destructive. Let us look at the story in Genesis 19, beginning in verse four. The angels had come to the city in the evening. Lot had met the two angels at the front gate of the city. He invited the two angels to stay at his home. Before they had turned in for the night, all the men of the city, both young and old, surrounded the house. In verse five they ask Lot to bring the men out to them so as to know them. Some translations say this means to have relations with them, but the true meaning is "to know." It is used over 943 times in Scripture and only in five places does it have sexual connotation—and then it is always a heterosexual issue and not a homosexual issue. The sexual activity here is that of rape. Rape itself is not a sexual act as much as it is an act of violence. This understanding is supported by II Peter 2:7, which refers to the "licentiousness" of the men of Sodom. It is hard to conceive that ALL the men and boys in Sodom were homosexuals. Whether in Biblical times or present day, homosexuals have always been a minority. There is no proof that Sodom was a totally homosexual society. What is obvious is that it was a society riddled with problems. Several passages in the old Testament, such as Ecclesiastes, say that God abhorred the Sodomites for their pride (16:8). In Ezekiel, the sins of Sodom are not only listed categorically, but also contrasted with the sexual sins of Jerusalem as less serious. But, nowhere are the sins specified as homosexuality. The sexual aspect of this story was not due to a sickness of deviant behavior. If we study ancient history from an eastern thinking and not a western understanding, the truth is known. It is a known fact that ancient warriors who were defeated in battle, would bow to humility by being forced to take the part of a woman and be passive recipients in anal intercourse. This issue had nothing to do with homosexuality. Therefore, what took place at Lot's house was not uncommon. The fact is that the people reminded Lot he was a stranger in their land. History also tells us that people, at that time, were not friendly to strangers coming into their city. The actions of ALL of the men and boys in the city were not a sexual issue. A closely related passage is found in Judges 19:22, which is strongly influenced by Genesis 19. In this story the Levite of Aphraim and his concubine are not able to find hospitality in Gibeah until an old man, a "foreign resident" just like Lot. The stories are parallels to one another. Again, homosexuality was not the issue. Inhospitality was. The whole homosexual saga has mistakenly been interpreted from the word Sodom, Sodomy, and Sodomite. In the King James Bible, the Old Testament implied sexual sins. If this translation were correct, it does not single out a particular sin. In the early seventeenth century sodomy referred to unnatural sex acts of any type. We have shown that Dr. Judd Marmor's studies show that homosexuality is not unnatural in the animal/mammal kingdom. The question we must ask ourselves is: "If these men who surrounded

Lot's house were gay, why did Lot offer his daughter, knowing this Fact?" Secondly, if ALL the men who surrounded the house were gay, what about the women and children? In understanding human sexuality we know the answers to these two questions. It is clear that the so-called scholars in the radical Christian churches cloud their thinking with a homophobic mentality.

UNDERSTANDING LEVITICUS 18:22 AND LEVITICUS 20:13

We come to yet another passage wherein the fundamentalists say homosexuality is a disgrace. However, again they fail to use the basic tools of interpretation, as discussed earlier. The basic concept of Leviticus 18:22 and Leviticus 20:13 is the issue that a man should not lie with another man as does a man with a woman. With this in mind, the fundamentalists clearly see homosexuality as forbidden. However, in this setting they fail to look at both the historical and synthesis principles. In Leviticus 18 it is specifically written to distinguish the Jews from the pagans among whom they had been living, or would live, as its opening remarks make clear. Although both chapters also contain prohibitions (e.g., against incest and adultery) which might seem to stem from moral absolutes, their function, in the context of Leviticus 18 and 20, are symbols of Jewish distinctiveness. The following are some thoughts regarding Leviticus 18:22 and Leviticus 20:13, which are important to totally understand these passages. Could be: Same sex between heterosexuals. Historically: conquering nations or leaders were to force conquered male into same sex anal intercourse with the conquering hero. Strongest: Pagan worship rites and heathen sexual practices to appease the nature of deities. Abomination: Throughout the Scriptures, this word refers to idol worship, and pagan rites and rituals. Historically: We know that male prostitutes were prevalent in ancient peoples' worship. In Leviticus 18:22 and 20:13, there is found a struggle between Law and Grace. Leviticus was written to God's people who were subject to the Law. But God's people today are not subject to the Law, but under Grace. The Jewish distinctions between intrinsic wrong and ritual impurity are better understood by the

Hebrew word, "Toevah." In its meaning "Toevah," does not signify something intrinsically evil, like rape or theft. In these passages the meaning shows something as ritually unclean as eating pork or engaging in intercourse during menstruation. The sad commentary of this passage is those within the radical Christian churches who feel homosexuals should be put to death. Can you imagine a young gay youth hearing this type of message come out of a church. The psychological and mental anguish they must endure by the radical Christian church. What is sad about the misinterpretations of these passages is that injunctions against homosexual acts are held valid today, but at the same time most other parts of the Holiness Code are deemed irrelevant. Should the death penalty be used against sex acts, between two men or women? Why are female same-sex acts not mentioned? What is the link between female subordination and the fear of sex between men both evident in these laws? There is no doubt an unhealthy understanding of sex and sexuality. These passages had nothing to do with homosexuality, but pagan worship. Also, the laws were set in particular, for the people of Israel who would not worship the one true God. Once again the focus of homosexuals is a case for bigotry and hatred towards a particular group. We know the results can be devastating to the person's being attacked by such hatred. It causes pain and suffering. It also takes years of counseling to bring about healing.

WHAT ABOUT THE CREATION STORY?

In this chapter, we will look at sexuality and procreation in light of Scripture. The fundamentalists have a rather narrow view of sexuality and procreation. Here, it is tradition they hold to—not the facts. Sex is a biologically based need, which centers not upon procreation, but towards pleasure and tension release. Sexuality has a broader understanding than sex. This explains the misconceptions the radical Christian churches have regarding homosexuality. Sexuality includes sex and relates to biological organ systems, sexuality distinguishes us as male or female. With this distinction, there are attitudes and characteristics, which are defined as masculine and feminine.

The attempt to draw the distinction between sex and sexuality is important and useful. Admittedly, however, it is a difficult distinction to maintain with clarity and consistency. The two terms are interdependent: one (sexuality) includes, but also depends upon, the other (sex). Moreover, we encounter the linguistic fact that both words have the same adjectival and adverbial forms. Still, it is crucial to bear in mind that sexuality involves much more than what we do with our genitals. More fundamentally, it is who we are as a body—selves who experience the emotional, cognitive, physical and spiritual need for intimate communion—human and divine. (p. 18, *Embodiment*).

In Genesis 1:27-28, we see where God made man and woman. Also, we see where procreation came into being.

"And God created man in His own image, in the image of God. He created him; male and female He created them. And God blessed them; and God said to them, "Be fruitful and multiply, and fill the earth, and subdue it; and rule over the fish of the sea, and over the birds of the sky, and over every living thing that moves on the earth." (Gen. 1:26-28).

It is from this passage that fundamentalist Christians throw up the procreation story as proof that gay relations are against God. They conclude that since it says that God made man and woman, that man and man or woman and woman are against God's standard. Again, we go back to the principles of interpretation in order to truly understand this passage. Genesis, chapter one, deals solely with procreation. It has nothing to do with sexuality in its broadest terms. Verse twenty-eight gives us God's purpose for making male and female. He needed them to populate the earth. This is only one aspect of God's plan. This does not take away the fact that He also made gay people. A person cannot (should not) take one line out of Scripture and build a belief around it, but rather should look at the whole of Scripture before coming to a conclusion. As we search the Scriptures in detail, we find many avenues to God's plan—a plan so advanced and magnificent that we simply could never understand it all. Those who are so narrow-minded to say that God made man and woman, not man and man, fail to see the big picture. We, who are gay, would agree that God made man and woman for the purpose of procreation. Yet, if we go to the New Testament, Paul talks about marriage and celibacy. In I Corinthians, Chapter 7, Paul begins the chapter by talking about husbands and wives. Then he goes on to talk about celibacy, which is against procreation altogether. In one sense it is a contradiction to God's plan outlined in Genesis, 1:28. This is what a narrow-minded person does: bring contradiction to Scriptures. But, when we look at the total plan of God, we see many different avenues. Some get married, some are celibate, and some are gay. The story in I Corinthians, Chapter 7, begins to unfold as Paul goes through the chapter and beings to take other avenues. Even though Chapter 7 of I Corinthians is dealing with marriage, it also builds upon other issues. Paul also makes a full statement as to our calling, which can have an effect on the other areas of a person's life.

> Only, as the Lord has assigned to each one, as God has called each, in this manner let him walk. And thus I direct in all the churches. Was any man called already circumcised? Let him not become uncircumcised. Has anyone been called in uncircumcision? Let him not be circumcised. Circumcision is nothing, and uncircumcision is nothing, but what matters is the keeping of the commandments of God. Let each man remain in that condition in which he was called. (p. 1736, *The Ryrie Study Bible*).

Paul alludes to circumcision, which has nothing to do with marriage, but he is making a statement which can be used in this situation or any other situation. We need to look more closely at the word, "Circumcision," which Paul used to make this point.

The English word is derived from the Latin and means literally, "to cut around." The Biblical reference is to an operation whereby the foreskin (prepuce), a covering of skin on the head of the penis of the male, is removed by surgery...In Biblical times, circumcision was practiced widely among the Western Semites, including the Hebrews. Numerous references suggest that circumcision became a mark of racial and cultural pride. The Philistines, and later the Greeks were derisively referred to as the "uncircumcised." (Judge 14:3; 15:18; I Sam. 14:6; 17:26; II Sam. 1:20; I Chron. 10:4; Acts 15:1; Gal. 5:1-12) (p. 866, The Zondervan Pictorial Encyclopedia of the Bible).

In Paul's case and during this time, circumcision distinguished between Jew and non-Jew. Paul is saying, whether circumcised or uncircumcised, it does not matter—it is where we are CALLED that is the issue. Paul alludes to the issue of marriage and its ramifications, but it can also be eluded to other issues of life; in this case, the gay lifestyle. Paul's principle can be applied to those of us who are gay. Whether gay or straight, (circumcised or uncircumcised), it is not the issue—but rather that we keep the commandments of God (I Cor. 7:19), and remain in the condition in which God has called us.

Were you called while a slave? Do not worry about it; but if you are able also to become free, rather do that. For he who was called in the Lord while a slave, is the Lord's freed man; likewise, he who was called while free, is Christ's slave. You were bought with a price; do not become slaves of men. Brethren, let each man remain with God in that condition in which he was called. (p. 1736, The Ryrie Study Bible).

The creation story is simply that: about creation. We have no problem with the fact that most creation is heterosexual...but that does not allow for other aspects of humanity. Through Scripture we see a diverse plan. The creation story is just one aspect of God's total plan. Furthermore, we must not forget to read the creation story in light of its historical setting. It was the beginning of beginnings. Procreation was in the mind of God when He created Adam and Eve. But that does not hinder or belittle the fact that God also made the Jonathans and the Davids. Within God's plan we see other types of relationships emerge and integrate. From this we can understand homosexuality in light of the creation story.

THE GREATEST LOVE STORY

The story of Jonathan and David is the greatest love story of all times. It is in I and II Samuel, that we see this love story between two men unfold. In chapter eighteen of I Samuel, you begin to see the kindled relationship between Jonathan and David. Their relationship was so close and beyond friendship. They were lovers who had made a covenant between themselves. Jonathan's father Saul, was angry with him and said: "You son of a perverse, rebellious woman. Do I not know that you are choosing the son of Jesse to your own shame and the shame of your mother's nakedness (I Sam. 20:30). It is only logical, that this anger and shame was because of their love relationship. This is supported by verse 41, where Jonathan and David kissed. This was not a friendly kiss, but a passionate kiss between them. It says, "They kissed until David exceeded (spilled his seed upon the ground). In II Samuel 1:26, we see this point even clearer, "Your love to me was more wonderful, than the love of women." The Hebrew word Ahab means to have a sexual affection, or in this case, it is used in response to a lover and a sexual action. To make this point more evident, if we go to the Septaugent of the Old Testament we find the word ahabah, which comes from the Greek word agapa to have affection. It also means love in a social or moral sense. The word in this passage is not phileo, which shows a brotherly love. The love between Jonathan and David was more than just as friends, but as lovers. It is important for gay Christians to see the healthy relationship of Jonathan and David. Also, it shows what they encountered. Their relationship did not last, because of David's position as next King. They might have kept their relationship a secret. The most important thing for gay Christians to know is their relationships are healthy and needed. Love between two people of the same gender is OK in God's eyes.

WHAT DID PAUL SAY ON THE SUBJECT?

Now we turn our thoughts to the New Testament. It seems that Paul was the only writer who had anything to say on the subject…or did he?

> Saint Paul, whose commitment to Jewish law had taken up most of his life, never suggested that there was any historical or legal reason to oppose homosexual behavior; if he did in fact contemporary moral standards. (p. 106, *Christianity, Social Tolerance and Homosexuality*).

We look at Romans 1:26, I Corinthians 6:9 and I Timothy 1:10. Also, we will look at other passages, which shed some light on the subject. Romans 1:26 is one of those passages the fundamentalists run to in order to make their point that homosexuality is sinful and wrong. It is this attitude, which has had a great effect upon gays and lesbians. Such belief, which says homosexuality is sinful and wrong causes many homosexuals to try and change their orientation. Yet when we look closely at Romans, Chapter One, we see the issue is not about homosexuality, but pagan worship.

> One of the most serious flaws found in expositions of Romans is the assumption that all homosexual activity is a manifestation of sexual perversion. This approach fails to take into account the very real and verifiable distinction in modern psychology between sexual perversion and sexual inversion. Perversion involves a conscious choice to take part in sexual activity that is opposed to the person's natural instincts. It is usually associated with psychological abnormality, and in the

view of scripture, is an indication of the deepest individual and societal corruption. Inversion, on the other hand, is the sexual orientation one discovers in oneself, quite apart from any conscious choice. It is a bias, integrated aspect of a person's total selfhood and sense of identity, which, while its cause and origin are not always explainable, is nevertheless a reality that will not go away; and despite all attempts, it has not been proven to be reversible. (p. 92, *Gays Under Grace*).

It has been proven that the deviation Paul had in mind was sexual perversion. It is a fact that in Paul's day, they had no understanding of sexual inversion. Let us go back to the book of Romans, Chapter One.

Verse 21—For even though they knew God, they did not honor Him as God, or give thanks, but they became futile in their speculations, and their foolish heart was darkened.

This passage says they KNEW GOD—they did not honor Him as God. It seems these people outwardly demonstrated love of God by their rituals, but in their hearts they did not know him. This is not true in regards to the gay Christian. They have come to understand God as holy and the One to be worshipped. Verse 23 and 24 show us the picture of those who did not know God, but knew of Him. These people did horrible things such as exchange the glory of God for corruptible man, birds, four-footed animals, and crawling creatures (pagan worship). Verses 26 and 27 are where the fundamentalists pin their theological conclusion regarding the whole chapter. Yet it is these two lines (women with women, men with men) that are picked to be used out of the entire chapter. The synthesis principle is being grossly violated. We must look at the whole chapter, not only two lines, to come to a theological conclusion.

Verse 26—For this reason, God gave them over to degrading passions; for their women exchanged the natural function for that which is unnatural.

The fundamentalists focus on "natural function for that which is unnatural," and say this proves that God is against homosexuals. Yet the passage is referring to heterosexual persons. There are two key words that prove this point.

NATURE:

For Paul, "nature" was not a question of universal law or truth, but rather a matter of the character of some person or groups of persons; a character which was largely ethnic and entirely human: Jews are Jews by nature, just as Gentiles are Gentiles by nature." It is not "nature" in the abstract, but someone's nature..."Nature" in Romans 1:26, then, should be understood as the personal nature of the pagans in question... Paul believed that the Gentiles knew of the truth of God but rejected it and likewise rejected their true "nature" as regarded by their sexual appetites, going beyond what was "natural" for them and what was approved for the Jews. (p. 96-97, *Gays Under Grace*).

THEIR:

Looking in verse 26, we see an important word, "their," which explains the verse clearly. It says, "their" women, whose women? The **men's** women. This does not give a picture of a homosexual, but a heterosexual. The people Paul is giving reference to are heterosexuals, not homosexuals. The issue is pagan worship not sex. It needs to be understood, that sex acts between two people of the same gender does not constitute homosexuality. The adjective "their," makes it very clear that Paul was talking to heterosexuals. It seems that just because sex was the issue, radical Christians assume that it was a homosexual issue. A homosexual is homosexual whether sex is involved or not. Those who see only sex are ignorant of sexuality. They also fail to read chapter one in its entirety. In verses 29 and 30 we see yet other characteristics:

Unrighteousness	Envy
Wickedness	Murder
Greed	Strife
Malice	Gossip
Slander	Haters of God
Insolence	Arrogance
Boastfulness	Inventors of evil
Disobedience to parents	Without understanding
Untrustworthiness	Unloving

As we look at the list above, we can think of many people in our churches who have these traits. It is obvious that Paul did not condemn homosexuals, nor was the passage centered around this issue at all. George Edwards puts it this way:

In the section, Romans 1:18-3:20, the need of all (Gentile and Jew) for grace of God is underlined. Verses 1:18-32 denounces Gentile unrighteousness along the lines found in Hellenistic Judaism, especially the Book of Wisdom, which repudiates Gentile religions as "foolish idolatries." God sends on the idolaters (Wisdom 11-12) punishments suited to the deeds. This is like the statement (Romans 1:18) that "the wrath of

God is revealed from heaven against all ungodliness and wickedness" or "the dishonorable passions," of Romans 1:26-27 to which God gives them up. Even a list of vices to match Romans 1:29-31 is found at Wisdom 14:25-26, "bloody murder, theft and fraud, corruption, treachery, riot, perjury, honest men driven to distraction, ingratitude, moral corruption, sexual perversion, breakdown of marriage, adultery, debauchery. All of these vices derive directly from idolatry." (Wisdom 14:27). (p. 73, *Gay/Lesbian Liberation*).

Another point of contention is I Corinthians 6:9. In this passage the fundamentalists say it clearly shows that homosexuals will not inherit the Kingdom of God. This is not consistent with the Gospel message. In some modern translations they insert the word homosexual, which is incorrect with the Greek word. The King James Bible, and back, does not insert the word homosexual, because the Greek language does not allow for it. Also, the word homosexual was not even coined until the late 1800's. The English language had two words, which denoted same sex relations, introvert and introsexual. Neither word appears in any of our English translations. There are two words needing translation. The first word is Malacost, which means soft or loose. The second word Arsenokoitai, which means man bed. The issue here was male prostitutes. In other languages such as German, it means child molester. In Italian it's a pervert. In French it's a person with bad habits. Only in modern English do some seek to translate it to mean homosexual, which is a mistranslation. It is sad how far bigotry will go to prove a point. The Jerusalem Bible translates effeminate catamites as:

> Catamites in the New Testament times were soft, young adolescent boys apprenticed usually to a married man of means who provided an education for his young protege in exchange for playful sexual use of the young boy's body. Nothing in history bears out that this practice in any way involved homosexuals. Rather, it was a social, more in common practice. (p. 141, *Good News for Modern Gays*).

The word arsenokoitai (abusers of themselves with mankind KJV) or as the Greek says, "Man Bed." In today's modern translations we seem to come with numerous words such as perverts, sodomites, sexually uncontrolled or perverted or pederasts (child molesters). It seems that today's translations cannot seem to find a clearly defined word.

> The second word, arsenokoitai, occurs once each in I Corinthians and I Timothy, but nowhere else in other literature of the period. It is derived from two Greek words, one meaning "males" and the other "beds," a euphemism for sexual intercourse. Other Greek words were commonly used to describe homosexual behavior, but do not appear here. The large context of I Corinthians 6, shows Paul extremely concerned with prostitution, so it is very possible he was referring to male prostitutes. But many experts, now attempting to translate these words, have reached a simple conclusion; their precise meaning is uncertain. (p. 7, *Homosexuality, Not a Sin/Not a Sickness*).

Another passage, which is greatly associated with I Corinthians 6:9, is found in I Timothy 1:10. Some say that the word arsenokoitai in I Corinthians 6:9, is the same word used in I Timothy 1:10. The two passages are similar, but not identical. The immoral persons in I Timothy 1:10, is the word in English for porno. It denoted male prostitutes.

> The Greek word has a vulgar connotation rather than "fucker of males" and applies not to same-sex intercourse between males, but to intercourse between males and females. This is premised on the assertion that copulation with other males would have been expressed with "arreno" rather than "arsenokoites." This argument runs aground on the fact that the spellings arr and ars occur without differentiation in the Oxyrhuynchus Papyri, in the Zenon Papyri, and in manuscripts of Biblical Greek. (p. 82, *Gay/Lesbian Liberation*).

Male prostitution is a service that has been around since the beginning of time. Male prostitution has never been set on any certain gender. Maury Johnston makes a very good statement.

> In the final analysis, what, then, can be said of the New Testament's understanding of homosexuality? As far as homosexual inversion is concerned, the Christian scriptures say absolutely nothing. It is certain, if not obvious from the writings themselves, that homosexual orientation, as we understand it today, in light of the complex psychological biological and sociological givens, was unknown by Christians of the early church. (p. 96-97, *Gays Under Fire*).

This chapter sought to answer the question regarding homosexuality and the Bible. The truths that have been set in these pages can set a gay or lesbian free from the entanglement of the radical Christian churches (fundamentalist). The Bible says the truth will set you free. In the same sense, the gay Christian can feel the freedom from oppression, damnation, condemnation and hatred. In doing so, they will begin the process toward psychological and spiritual wholeness. Most gays have felt this oppression, damnation, condemnation and hatred for years. The healing process will take some time. It does not happen overnight. Again, the reason for this chapter is to show how much damage the Bible can cause any certain group when its pages are misinterpreted due to ignorance or stupidity. In either case, we need to think about the results that come from bigotry and hatred. Such homophobic behavior has had devastating results that have led to many deaths. In closing this chapter, we leave you with a gift.

DID YOU KNOW…

That your orientation (Straight or Gay) has nothing to do with SALVATION?

JESUS CHRIST is the only way to Eternal Life in Heaven (John 14:6)?

All (EVERYONE) has sinned and fallen short of God's glory (Romans 3:23)?

The wages of our sin is death, both physically and spiritually (Romans 6:23)?

But CHRIST died for our sins as payment (Romans 5:8)?

HOW CAN YOU BE SAVED?

Confess "Jesus is Lord" and believe in your heart God raised Jesus from the dead (John 3:16-18; Romans 10:9-10; Acts 16:31).

Nowhere does the BIBLE or JESUS CHRIST condemn or damn Gays/Lesbians (John 3:17; Matt. 10:11-15). It is here we see God's Mercy, Forgiveness and Love, which is the Gospel Message.

The hope for Gay/Lesbian Christians is in Jesus Christ and not in man. The Apostle Paul puts it this way:

> "For I am convinced that neither death, nor life, nor angels, nor principalities, not things present, nor things to come, nor powers, nor height, nor depth, nor any other created thing, shall be able to separate me from the Love of God, which is in CHRIST JESUS my LORD." (Romans 8:38-39).

Boy, that says it all. It is a promise to all Christians (Gay, Straight, Black or White). The gay Christian needs to know that Jesus Himself mentioned the Sodom and Gomorrah story, but never mentioned homosexuality. Jesus did mention inhospitality. If the lifestyle of homosexuality is judgment/damnation as the fundamentalists put it, then Jesus would have been sure to make issue of an important issue such as homosexuality. The fact being, that homosexuality was not an issue with the Lord Jesus Christ, proves this chapter's point. You see, God made gays and lesbians the wonderful people who make up a segment of this place we call Earth.

May this chapter bring you hope and healing. May the truths in this chapter begin to change your old thoughts of myths and misconceptions about your sexuality. As you instill these truths, your thoughts will gain new entrance into your psychological and spiritual wellbeing. This will allow you to soar to new heights, where you have been oppressed. May the feelings that have been buried behind closed doors come out into the light. The truth will set you free.

Chapter 5

Confusion Leads to Chaos

The radical Christian churches have an unhealthy understanding of sex and human sexuality. In this chapter, I will share some of my own story regarding this chaos. In another chapter we talk about the Ex-gay Movement, which causes chaos, in the fact that they allude to their techniques that cure homosexuals—that with God's help they can become healthy heterosexuals. Some of the ex-gay groups have changed their overtone on this issue, to say that a homosexual may not be able to change, but must not act on their true feelings. In the radical Christian's view, these feelings are sinful. The story that will be told about one such ex-gay leader shows us the identity crisis that occurs when a person seeks to change their orientation. On several occasions, I have had the opportunity to challenge the Ex-gay Movement on their thoughts regarding homosexuality and their success rate of changing gays and lesbians to healthy heterosexuals. As of today, there are no studies to prove their success rate, but we do see the chaos, which comes out of such groups. My own life in an ex-gay ministry proves my point. The fact that I tried every avenue possible to change my homosexual feelings. In my work today with gays and lesbians, I receive many calls and letters from ex-gay people whose lives are in total chaos. If they thought they had an identity crisis going into an ex-gay group, it was heightened when they left the group a failure. I had the.opportunity to meet Colin Cook, an ex-gay minister, on the Phil Donahue show. Before the show started, Colin Cook came up to me and introduced himself and proceeded to talk about bestiality. This was my first clue he assumed all homosexuals were into bestiality. I assumed this must be his sexual fantasy. It was amazing to observe the guests on the platform with me. Their body language and answers to my questions said it all. I remember Colin Cook's wife held onto him for dear life. Oh yes, she wanted the world to know her husband was cured of his homosexuality. Throughout the program, Colin and the other guests said they no longer struggled with homosexual tendencies. That God had healed them of this sinful behavior. I remember saying the same things as a Baptist minister. This alone can cause psychological and mental anguish. It does give a false identity to a person. Every ex-gay who has been in my office states they have never overcome their homosexual feelings. It was a daily struggle to keep the feelings hidden. It is no wonder that gays and lesbians are faced with an identity crisis. When such people as Colin Cook give false hope and lies about gays and lesbians being able to change their orientation through counseling and prayer, it causes damage. For example, someone might have watched that program on the Phil Donahue Show and saw hope in changing his or her sinful homosexuality. I wonder how many were not able to change their orientation and committed suicide? In some cases it lead to marriage, which in most cases, ends in divorce. Because of their guilt and shame many find no way out, but to drink or take drugs. For many Christians who struggle with homosexuality, it leads to bathhouses, book stores and prostitution. We see the domino effect, caused by negative and false statements regarding homosexual feelings. The whole misunderstanding of homosexuality goes back in history.

> But we are a particularly sexophobic nation. Much of this can be traced to our Puritan ancestry. We fear sex so terribly, that we literally cripple if not destroy the natural emerging sexuality of our children. Most people can't cope with the fact that

children are born sexual. As John Money points out, little boys have as many as three erections every twenty-four hours. Like wise, little girls experience vaginal lubrication from infancy on. (p. 70, *Homosexuals and Sexuality*).

It is the whole Western thinking of sex as dirty, and we do not talk about it, especially homosexuality. Society has shaped our understanding of sexuality, which has had an effect upon the understanding of homosexuality.

Recent work on the historical-cultural construction of sexuality brings definition to the cultural factors, which shape sexual behavior, and in a sense, chips away at the essential core by establishing the importance of external, social factors. (p. 5, *An Anthropology and Homosexual Behavio*r).

It will be through education that Western society will begin to see a healthier side to sexuality. In seeing a positive side to human sexuality, we will be able to see its diversity. In this case, homosexuality will shed greater light on the complexity of human sexuality. This misconception about sex being a dirty word will change as we go beyond the sex organ. Again, sex goes beyond the radical Christians' view of procreation. There is more to sex than children. Also, there are some differences between sex and sexuality. For example, a homosexual orientation does not depend upon what a person does in bed. There are many other factors, which denote a homosexual orientation, such as social behavior, genetic, and hormonal. Also, education about sex and sexuality should not begin in adulthood. It should begin in childhood.

It is especially appropriate because the most intensive period during which the child learns spoken language coincides with the most intensive phase of sexual learning—between the ages of 1-1/2 or 2 to 5 years. By the time the child is 5, it has done the most intensive sexual learning of his/her entire life. By age 5, in other words, the child's developing sexuality has either been nurtured or crippled, often prematurely. (p. 70, *Homosexuals & Sexuality*).

Our Western Society has greatly crippled the child's sexual development, because of this narrow view of sexuality. In the case of gays and lesbians this point shows us two things:

1) That their homosexuality is not something learned, since by the age of five the child has done the most intensive sexual learning of their entire life.

2) Because of the radical Christians' misconceptions about homosexuality, it has not only crippled the gays and lesbians growth, but also caused an identity crisis. This is seen in our ex-gay ministries who try to change homosexuals. They psychologically damage through various therapies, which seek to change homosexual orientation.

In recent months the ex-gay movement has been in the news as they seek to spread their message that gays and lesbians can become heterosexual. But people like myself who have come out of such groups can tell you it does not work. Back in 1993 I was a guest on the Phil Donahue Show debating with the leaders of some of the ex-gay groups. It was sad to see them lying on national television that they did not struggle with homosexuality any more. One of those guests was Colin Cook who headed up Homosexuals Anonymous and a counseling service to help gay men come out of homosexuality. Unfortunately, he was discovered to have been having phone sex and sex with his clients in his office. Since the finding of these facts Colin's wife who was on the Phil Donahue show was just as much in denial about her husband's homosexuality as he was. It is amazing how the dysfunction of such denial affects not only the person struggling with their homosexuality, but those closest to them. In Colin's case, his wife left him and told the newspapers that she did not realize the struggle of homosexuality was so hard to overcome. The fact is, you cannot change your orientation no more than you can change an apple into an orange. It is impossible, but if you do succeed at making any change it is like creating Frankenstein. So many gay and lesbian Christians coming out of the closet and realizing God loves them for who they are is having a great effect upon the ex-gay movement. Many ex-gay groups have shut their doors and many more on the way out. Thank God for this change of events. There are many ex-gays, including myself who have finally stood up and said changing your orientation does not work, and God never intended for it to be. Most of those who try to change their orientation either come out of a radical Christian church or were not homosexual from the beginning. Again, in the study of sexuality we realize that almost everyone does experiment with his or her orientation, which could be same gender sex. Freud himself considered all human beings to be born BI-sexual and find their place in sexuality as they begin to grow. We know that sexual orientation is found early in life and before any sexual contact, that of homosexual or heterosexual. So, for people like Colin Cook, we must realize they are confused about who they are. As a Christian we must realize that our orientation has nothing to do with our salvation. We are wonderfully made no matter what our orientation.

Colin Cook is in denial about his homosexuality. He is just one of many so-called ex-gays in denial. This all stems from the radical Christian churches, which say homosexuality is sinful. Unfortunately, many gay Christians find themselves trying to change their orientation, which begins the chaos. The war that goes on between mind, body and spirit. Many gays and lesbians take on a dual personality— it's the only way they can hide their sexual feelings and attitudes. For example, at work they put on the straight act and at play, they let their hair down and let themselves be gay. Those who are in this situation live with fear of being found out; they also feel the oppression of not letting their feelings be true to themselves. Most ex-gays are confused about their sexuality. On one hand they are told to suppress their homosexual feelings and yet they cannot rid those feelings which are normal. The ex-gay movement would have them believe their feelings are not natural, since God created them male and female. Carl Jung made this statement regarding those who came to see him with sexual questions. These questions turned out to have an inevitable religious flavor. The radical Christian movement has an effect upon its people's understanding of sexuality and sex.

> The Christian heritage contains not only a plethora of teachings concerning sexual morality; it also bears great theological themes of sexual relevance. What we believe about creation and God's purpose in creating us as sexual beings, what we believe about human nature and destiny, what we believe about sin and salvation, about love, justice and community— these and many other basic beliefs will condition and shape our sexual self-understandings. (p. 14-15, *Embodiment*).

This is seen in the gays and lesbians who have a strong Christian belief system. Those gays and lesbians who have found freedom in their sexuality are able to overcome the radical Christians narrow view of human sexuality.

> In looking at various parts of the Christian tradition, we will find it relatively easy to observe how frequently an incarnational understanding of sexuality was lost and how often sinful patterns of domination and submission in human relationships were assumed to arise out of divine decree. But the errors detected in others should remind us that a "definitive" interpretation of God's work in human sexuality is a chimerical quest. (p. 16, *Embodiment*).

The sexual dysfunction found in our churches causes the chaos we find in the Ex-gay Movement. If only they would embrace their sexuality as a homosexual. This is why such people as Colin Cook find themselves in turmoil. The issue goes beyond the gay Christian. We saw Jimmy Swaggart, the great television Evangelist, having sex with prostitutes. The point is, any type of sexual dysfunction leads to chaos.

Sexuality (heterosexual or homosexual) is a wonderful part of who we are, which experiences the emotional, cognitive, physical and spiritual need for close communion with man and God.

> Sexuality is a sign, a symbol, and a means of our call to communication and communion. This is most apparent in regard to other human beings, other body-selves. The mystery of our sexuality is the mystery or need to reach out to embrace others both physically and spiritually. Sexuality thus expresses God's intention that we find our authentic humanness in relationship. But such humanizing relationship cannot occur on the human dimension alone. Sexuality, we must also say, is intrinsic to our relationship with God. (p. 18, *Embodiment*).

This cycle is broken with the gay Christian. Not only do they have a misconception about their own identity, but also with God. Through such churches as The Atlantic Association of Christian Churches, the gay Christian can begin to put their life, sexuality, and spirituality back together again. There are many out there whose lives are in chaos. Not only is the person who is struggling with their orientation hurting, but also their families who do not know. The pain and suffering goes on for years until the gay person comes out of the closet, only then, does the pain begin to heal. The road to that process is not easy. The answers are not patent. Those who say they have changed, but in reality have not, have the greatest pain. Having met Colin Cook, I understand his telling the world he no longer struggled with homosexual feelings. He wanted the world to know that Jesus had changed those feelings to heterosexual feelings. What lies we tell in the name of God's love to us. If only those within the Ex-gay Movement would realize that God made them to love themselves as gays and lesbians. That God does not make junk, or make mistakes. Again, we can try to change our thoughts, which in this case leads to brainwashing. Such mind control happens a lot in religious circles. We can change the behavior by getting married, which many gays and lesbians have with no success. As you read Colin Cook's story, you will see a lot of counter-transference going on. It is important to understand counter-transference. The Dictionary of Pastoral Care and Counseling gives us a good definition:

> Exaggerated positive and negative feelings, fantasies and behavior in the counselor or therapist that are "transferred" from some other, earlier relationship (in contract to the client's "transference" reactions to the therapist). Some contemporary writers use the term to refer to all of the counselor's feelings and reactions to clients. (p. 239).

Again, as you read Colin's story you can see the counter-transference going on. The sad thing is that Colin played it out in therapy with other men struggling with their orientation. The struggle was that if they did not change, God would hate them for acting out on their feelings and send them to Hell. That alone is very damaging and causes people to doubt their sexuality and make changes.

Chapter 6

Homophobic Affects on Gays and Lesbians

In this chapter, we want to look at the effects of homophobia on gays and lesbians. Throughout this chapter we will look at words which cause the psychological and spiritual breakdown of gays and lesbians. Such words can have life affecting results and even death. The myths coming out of the radical Christian churches is one of the key reasons for homophobia. It is their fear of the unknown, which brings about bigotry and hatred. Some of those in the Christian church do so out of ignorance, because they do not understand. On the other hand, the leaders of these churches should know better, therefore their actions are based upon stupidity. We can only begin to understand the anguish that gays and lesbians face in coming out to the world. In coming-out, we have seen those who lost their job or career, lost their home, and family and friends. This type of reaction can cause gays and lesbians to stay in the closet. It is the worst place for a gay and lesbian to find themselves. Those who come from the radical Christian churches have an added dilemma, because they are told God hates their homosexuality and they are going to Hell. These two statements can bring a lot of emotions to a gay Christian. The damage caused by their brothers and sisters in Christ can have a lifetime effect. The pain caused to gay Christians leaves scars that may not heal. The wounds are so deep, that there seems to be no light ahead. Some feel like the sheep led to the slaughter. Some come out as survivors as others fall in defeat. The ones defeated may not physically end their life, but spiritually they do. The following words have a negative effect upon a person's decision to stay in the closet.

FEAR—The first thing a gay person feels when they realize they are a homosexual is fear of being found out. Can you image the mental torture one goes through in the midst of the coming-out process. It needs to be noted that coming-out begins with the person accepting their orientation, which does not denote coming-out to the world. The fear can stop this process. Any time we stop a cycle from taking its course can cause damage to a person's psychological and spiritual well being. The American Heritage Dictionary gives us an understanding of the word FEAR:

> A feeling of alarm or disquiet caused by the expectation of danger, pain, disaster, or the like; terror; dread; apprehension. An instance or manifestation of such a feeling. A state or condition of alarm or dread: The prisoners spent the night in fear. Extreme reverence or awe, as toward a supreme power. A ground for dread or apprehension; possibility of danger—for fear of. So as to prevent or avoid: She tiptoed for fear of waking the children. (p. 480).

The definition is a mouthful. When a gay person realizes they are different from social norms (homosexual) the fear rushes in. If they go to a radical Christian church the fear is heightened. Instead of facing the fear they seek to change their feelings by going to an ex-gay group. Some put their feelings so far into their subconscious. There are those who seek acceptance by getting married in hopes the feelings will go away. Boy, what a roller coaster ride the emotions take in a gay person's life. What helps subside the fear in any issue is education. The more we know about the subject and ourselves, the fear begins to go away. Fear can be a positive emotion in our lives. It is when it consumes us and does not allow us to be who we are, then it is a problem. It is the helplessness feeling that can be damaging to a person's psychological and spiritual well being. Those gays and lesbians who come to accept and understand their orientation are able to control their fear. There will always be those who do not accept or understand homosexuality. Once a gay person is able to take control of their own life can they alleviate the fear.

GUILT—The radical Christian churches are noted for their guilt trips on people. Using the Bible as their source supports the basis of their guilt. Those gays who come to church are given the guilt trip. For example they are told they must seek counseling, God's forgiveness and change their evil ways. When a gay person does not change their ways, they are told they are living in sin and going to Hell. That's a lot of guilt to place on someone who is coming to grips with who they are. Those who are Christians, but have very little Bible knowledge on the subject, can be confused. The guilt can be so overwhelming and consuming to the gay Christian. The American Heritage Dictionary puts it this way:

> The fact of being responsible for an offense or wrongdoing. Guilty behavior. Remorseful awareness of having done something wrong. Culpability for a crime or lesser breach of regulations. (p. 585).

Is loving a person of the same sex so wrong? How can loving any person be so wrong? Yet, the radical Christian churches would have gays and lesbians feel they have done something wrong. They seek to bring guilt upon anyone in their churches who do not change their wicked ways (homosexual feelings). The only way the person knows how to change their homosexual feelings is by hiding their feelings in an ex-gay group. In such groups they are convinced that God can change their homosexual feelings. Using a form of brainwashing, the Ex-gay groups convince their new converts that God has taken their homosexual feelings away. The gay Christian wants so badly to be rid of the guilt that they hide their true feelings deep within their being. They believe the lie to end their pain and suffering. In the end the Ex-gays find themselves struggling with their homosexual feelings, which some say is the devil trying to tempt them into sin. The guilt played out in our churches is a control factor, which destroys many lives. It is a false guilt that seeks only conformity. It has nothing to do with honesty and truth, which the Bible talks a lot about. The guilt used by the radical Christian churches is that of deception and wrong-doing. It is a false hope of no return.

> "Guilt is at the basis of much human suffering. I'll never get used to it," one counselor has said. "There is no box big enough to hold all the persons with guilt. (p. 11, *Counseling and Guilt* Earl D. Wilson Waco, Texas: Word 1987).

The radical Christian church does not help in this matter. Much of their behavior towards gays and lesbians is due to their fear of the unknown. The ignorance is not needed in today's world. Some of the so-called ignorance is stupidity surrounded with bigotry. We know that bigotry is not something we are born with, but something we learn. Therefore, what we learn can be changed, if we are seeking truth. The guilt used by the radical Christian churches is that which seeks to arouse feelings in people such as gays and lesbians. It has nothing to do with right or wrong. They seek to arouse unhealthy guilt feelings and tend to be manipulative. It is changing something which does not need changing. Changing the course causes psychological and spiritual havoc. One counselor puts it this way:

> Since the Bible never talks about subjective guilt feelings, in no place does it imply that we should try to arouse guilt feelings in others. In spite of this, many well-intentioned parents, teachers, preachers, television evangelists and counselors attempt to stir up guilt on the assumption that this will moti-vate others, stimulate Christian growth, punish wrongdoers, prevent pride, protect people from future sin, or stimulate financial contributions. (p. 136, *Christian Counseling* Gary R. Collins).

Those well-intentioned Christians do not realize the damage they cause in playing God. They seek to place guilt upon gays and lesbians by their misguided understanding of the Bible. Where the ball of emotions of guilt fall we cannot always know. In the gay and lesbian Christian it can lead to a low self-esteem, hate, confusion and anxiety. There is the self-condemning feelings, which a gay Christian feels, which brings about inferiority, inadequacy, weakness, pessimism and insecurity. All over the misuse of guilt and understanding of homosexuality. Out of the guilt comes physical tension and moral pain. It has no place in the development of gays and lesbians. It only hinders the growth cycle and mental well being of an individual.

SHAME—It is not uncommon for a person who suffers from guilt to also feel shame. This is seen a lot in our radical churches, who preach condemnation and damnation against homosexuality. Therefore those Christians dealing with homosexuality usually feel shame for their feelings, which their church says are not normal. The radical Christian churches would have gay Christians believe that their feeling toward someone of the same sex is sinful. The feelings are the devil's work, therefore they need to resist the temptation. This is what many gay Christians face in the coming-out process. It is such things as shame, which can hinder this process, therefore cause all sorts of havoc and psychological problems. The American Heritage Dictionary gives the following definition regarding shame:

> A painful emotion caused by a strong sense of guilt, embarrassment, unworthiness, or disgrace; A person or thing that brings dishonor, disgrace, or condemnation. (p. 1190).

For gays and lesbians it is a painful emotion, which has a lasting effect on their lives. It takes years to end the guilt, feeling unworthy and condemned for being gay. Many times they are disgraced from their families, friends and church. This is a lot for any person to handle. Again, some never recover. Those who recover, do so with a lot of hard work.

CONDEMNATION—This is the biggest action taken against gays and lesbians for their lifestyle. A feeling of condemnation has had the greatest effect upon gays and lesbians. In our earlier chapters you saw where some radical Christians were in agreement to have gay and lesbians put to death, which they seek to back up with scripture. What a sad commentary. No life is worth putting to death, because they seek to LOVE someone of the same gender. The concept of condemnation gives the feeling of doom. Many gays and lesbians who come out of the closet look doom in the face. The battle to win over condemnation has a price. For those gays and lesbians who ended their life because of condemnation, we remember their fight to the end. May their sudden exit out of life wake us up in this country, that bigotry is not the answer.

Gay Christians are told by their churches that they do not have to fall into temptation. Even with the struggle they can trust Christ to have victory over the sin of homosexuality. It is no wonder that most gays and lesbians feel guilty and dirty about their love towards a person of the same gender. This is one man's story:

> I dealt with this discovery alone. I never told anyone about my "sexual identity." I was so afraid of rejection. I remember rejection in seventh grade when all the other kids called me "fag" and "queer." No one even knew about me at that time; I couldn't bear to think how they would react if they really did know. All through high school and most of college I kept my secret—and my pain—to myself. (p. 278 *Christian Counseling*. Gary Collins).

No one should have to live in the closet. Secondly, should not have to deal with their coming-out alone. Thirdly, should not have to suffer the emotions mentioned above. The story above is just one of many. Hopefully, we can change such stories in the future.

Chapter 7

Homosexuality and Therapy

In this chapter, we will look at several therapies which say they have good results in treating homosexuality. The objective in these therapies is to change the sexual orientation of a homosexual to heterosexuality. There are very few sex therapists or psychotherapists who still believe that homosexuality can be treated. The few therapists that believe homosexuality can be treated are usually associated with the radical Christian movement. We will look at their modes of therapy. Their approach is mainly intended to help a homosexual who may, out of religious conviction, want to cease being a homosexual. Their goal is to help the homosexuals find their heterosexual side. In recent years, due to the facts of a genetic link, the radical Christian movement has accepted homosexuality as a disease. Even with this shift, many radical Christians still seek to change homosexuals into heterosexuals. In either case, we seek to show that such therapies are merely helping homosexuals repress their true homosexual orientation.

I. CONVERSION THERAPY—This therapy at one time was the treatment of homosexuality. During the time when homosexuality was considered an illness the choice of treatment was Conversion Therapy. Looking at this therapy we will see there has been no evidence to show this type of treatment was effective for its intended purpose. We will show that such therapy can be potentially harmful to a client. Trying to change homosexuals is not something new. For over a century religious professionals have sought to change the sexual orientation of homosexuals.

> Early attempts to reverse sexual orientation were founded on the unquestioned assumption that homosexuality is an unwanted, unhealthy condition. Although homosexuality has long been absent from the taxonomy of mental disorders, efforts to reorient gay men and lesbians persist. Recently for example, a coalition of mental health practitioners formed an organization dedicated to the "rehabilitation" of gay men and lesbians. Many practitioners still adhere to the officially debunked "illness" model of homosexuality, and many base their treatments on religious proscriptions against homosexual behavior. Still others defend sexual reorientation therapy as a matter of free choice for the unhappy client, claiming that their treatments do not imply a negative judgement on homosexuality, per se. They seek to provide what they describe as a treatment alternative for men and women whose homosexuality is somehow incongruent with their values, life goals, or psychological structures. (p. 221, *The Practice and Ethics of Sexual Orientation Conversion Therapy*).

The alternative given by the radical Christian movement is based upon the fear tactic, that homosexuality is sick, perverted, and a sin. This alone is enough for a gay Christian to seek change. Without the change God will not show favor on them. Their destination, ultimately will be Hell, unless they change their deviant behavior. Thank God, that many gay Christians have seen beyond the radical Christian movement's thinking of homosexuality. Conversion Therapy fails to define homosexuality, which is the first problem. It would seem, if Conversion Therapy is the answer, it would have addressed the question of how sexual orientation is defined. Having an understanding would be necessary before one can describe how sexual orientation is changed.

Several complex questions involved in the defining of sexual orientation have been either reduced or overlooked in the literature on conversion therapy. For instance, those conversion therapy programs that claim the greatest success included more subjects whose behavioral histories and fantasy lives appeared to have significant heteroerotic components (Haldeman, 1991). Instructing a "homosexual" subject with a priori heteroerotic responsiveness in heterosexual behavior appears to be easier than replacing the cognitive sociosexual schema and redirecting the behavior of the "homosexual" subject with no reported heteroerotic inclinations. Nevertheless, both types of "homosexual" subjects are often included in the same treatment group. Any definition of sexuality based solely on behavior is bound to be deficient and misleading. Sense of identity, internalized sociocultural expectations and importance of social and political affiliations all help define an individual's sexual orientation, and these variables may change over time. (p. 221 *The Practice and Ethics of Sexual Orientation Conversion Therapy*).

As stated earlier, we cannot base sexual orientation solely on behavior. For example there are those married people who later in life come out of the closet as a homosexual. They speak about their life struggle to be a heterosexual, because of society and religious beliefs. Conversion Therapy rests on its ability to understand who is being changed and its ability to describe the nature of the conversion happening. Another problem with conversion therapy is its inability to explain the complexities and ambiguities of sexual orientation. This leaves the question whether or not conversion therapy is effective. Psychotherapeutic approaches to homosexuality in this area do not leave room for acceptance of a homosexual orientation. Those who support a sexual orientation in homosexuals give two supporting hypotheses. The first is that homosexuality stems from a normal development or from pathological attachment patterns in early life.

The second is that homosexuality stems from faulty learning. The basis of their foundation is related to the dysfunction of the family. Their belief is based on clinical speculation and has never been empirically validated.

> Psychoanalytic treatment of homosexuality is exemplified by the work of Bieber et al. (1962), who advocate intensive, long-term therapy aimed at resolving the unconscious anxiety stemming from childhood conflicts that supposedly cause homosexuality. Beiber et al. saw homosexuality as always pathological and incompatible with a happy life. Their methodology has been criticized for use of an entirely clinical sample and for basing outcomes on subjective therapist impression, not externally validated data or even self-report. Follow-up data have been poorly presented and not empirical in nature. (p. 3, *The Practice and Ethics of Sexual Orientation Conversion Therapy*).

Such therapists have not shown a large percentage of change in their clients. Many of their clients were bisexual. Again the question is asked as to who is being converted, and what is the nature of the conversion. Those who are so-called converted spend a lifetime of struggling, which the radical Christian movement labels as our sin nature. If they have been truly converted there would be no struggle. If they have been healed there would be no need of a struggle. There are many gay Christians who do not struggle with their homosexuality, because they have overcome the radical Christians' viewpoint of homosexuality.

REPARATIVE THERAPY—This viewpoint is the latest therapy. A psychologist in California developed this theory by the name of Joseph Nicolosi. This therapy is used extensively in Ex-gay groups. In Dr. Joseph Nicolosi's book titled *Reparative Therapy of Male Homosexuality*, he makes some statements in his introduction which need corrections.

All three great pioneers of psychiatry—Freud, Jung, and Adler—saw homosexuality as pathological. Yet today, homosexuality is not to be found in the psychiatric manual of mental disorders (DSM-III-R) (p. 5, *Reparative Therapy of Male Homosexuals*).

This statement is not true. Freudianism does not see homosexuality as pathological or an illness. Freud wrote comparatively little about homosexuality. Freud thought that all people have latent homosexual tendencies. Therefore, Freud took a neutral stance on homosexuality. Freud wrote a letter to a mother of a gay son:

Homosexuality is assuredly no advantage but is nothing to be ashamed of, no vice, no degradation, it cannot be classified as an illness. Many highly respected individuals of ancient and modern times have been homosexuals, several of the greatest men, among them Plato, Michelangelo, Leonardo da Vinci, etc. It is a great injustice to persecute homosexuality as a crime and cruelty, too. (Masters, Johnson, and Kolodny, 1986) (p. 169, *Gay & Lesbian Mental Health*).

Are we going to say that such people like Plato, Michelangelo and Leonardo da Vinci, Martina Navratilova, Eleanor Roosevelt, Anna Freud and Ellen DeGeneres, according to Dr. Nicolosi, are all pathological? History as we have seen does not support his viewpoint. Remember that Freud himself at one point said that "homosexuality cannot be classified as an illness (pathological) (Jones 1955: 3, 208.)" (p. 222 Homo. A Philosophical Inquiry, Michael Ruse). Dr. Nicolosi does not stop with Freud. He goes on to talk about homosexual relationships.

Taking a look at gay relationships, we see there are many inherent limitations in same-sex love. Gay couplings are known for their volatility and instability. Research consistently reveals great promiscuity and a strong emphasis on sexuality in gay relationships. Without the stabilizing element of

the feminine influence, male couples have a great deal of diffi-
culty maintaining monogamy. (p. XVII, *Reparative Therapy of
Male Homosexuality*).

First, there is no consistent research showing the promiscuity in gay
relationships. It has only been in the last 15 years that homosexuals
have begun to come out of the closet. There are many lasting relationships in gay couples just like straight couples. But there are many couples (straight or gay), which end up braking apart, because of adultery
etc. Fact is that over 50% of all marriages end up in divorce. Therefore,
relationships on all levels show volatility, instability and promiscuity.
It has nothing to do with a person's sexual orientation. Dr. Nicolosi
believes that homosexuality on any level cannot be healthy and says
the homosexual identity can never be completely ego-syntonic (p. 13).

This belief erroneously presupposes a unitary gay lifestyle, a
concept more reductionist than that of sexual orientation. It
also prejudicially and without empirical justification assumes
that homosexual oriented people can never be normal or
happy. (p. 3, *The Practice of Ethics of Sexual Orientation
Conversion Therapy*).

Dr. Nicolosi's theory goes back to the father-son relationship of
homosexuals, which is the pathological assessment of homosexuality.
He feels that if you repair the family dynamics of the homosexual you
will begin to see the change towards heterosexuality in homosexuals.

The error in such reasoning is that the conclusion has pre-
ceded the data. There may be cause to examine the potentially harmful impact of a detached father and his effect on
the individual's self-concept or capacity for intimacy, but
why should a detached father be selected as the key player in
causing homosexuality, unless a priori decision about the
pathological nature of homosexuality has been made and
unless he is being investigated as the cause? This perspective

is not consistent with available data, nor does it explain the millions of heterosexual men who come from backgrounds similar to those of gay men, or for that matter, those gay men with strong father-son relationships. Nicolosi does not support his hypothesis or his treatment methods with any empirical data (p. 3, *The Practical & Ethics of Sexual Orientation Conversion Therapy*).

There are many stories about those who have said that Conversion and Reparative therapy does not help in changing one's homosexual orientation. The foundation of these therapies is based on a religious conviction. We will share with you two such stories. The biggest blow to Ex-Gay Movements was when Michael Bussee and Gary, former counselors with Exodus International (an Ex-Gay ministry), after 11 years of seclusion, the two original founders of Exodus International went public to denounce such programs that seek to convert homosexuals to heterosexuality. They said they counseled hundreds of people who tried to change their sexual orientation and none of them were successful. Also wondered how many of their clients went on to be committed, because of the guilt they heaped on them. Michael and Gary are just two of many ex-gays who realize somewhere along the way, that they did not change their orientation. Because of their love for the church they lied about their change to heterosexuality. The ex-gay movement gives studies to show their point of change, but the professionals do not support it.

Group treatments have also been used in sexual reorientation. One study of 32 subjects reports a 37% shift to heterosexuality (Hadden, 1966), but the results must be viewed with some skepticism, because of the entirely self-report nature of the outcome measures. Individuals involved in such group treatments are especially susceptible to the influence of social demand in their own reporting treatment success. Similarly, a study of 10 gay men resulted in the therapist's impressionistic claims that homosexual patients were able to "increase contact" with heterosexuals (Mintz 1966). Birk (1980) described a combination insight-oriented-social-learning-group format for treating homosexuality. He claimed that overall, 38% of his patients achieved "solid heterosexual shifts." Nonetheless, he acknowledges that these shifts represent "an adaptation to life, not a metamorphosis," and that homosexual fantasies and activity are ongoing, even for the "happily married" individual (Dirk, 198 p. 387). If a solid heterosexual shift is defined, as one is which a happily married person may engage in more than occasional homosexual encounters, perhaps this method is best described as a laboratory for heterosexual behavior, rather than a change of sexual orientation. (p. 4, *The Practice and Ethics of Sexual Orientation Conversion Therapy*).

Dr. Nicolosi collected case stories of homosexual men who experienced his "reparative" psychotherapy and put them into his book. What do the professionals say about his theory?

The APA said there was no scientific proof that the technique works and there is potential for harm. It now requires members to gain "informed consent" from patients by first advising them that being gay is not an illness, and that there are no proven benefits as well as potential risks to the therapy. (TWN August 20, 1997).

How dangerous are the therapies coming out of the radical Christian movement? As stated earlier, they are very dangerous. The following story says it all:

"One of my pet peeves is people who say of gays, "Well, if you people want to choose to be like that…" I did not choose to be this way. Most of us did not choose to be this way. It's just the way we are. We did not choose to be gay any more than heterosexuals choose to be 'straight'. It's just the way we are by nature. "Many of us have desired and wished and prayed to be changed, but as far as I can learn we cannot change or be changed either by psychology, psychiatry, or religion. Most people who thought they were changed by any of these means soon found that they were still gay. I would like to tell you one of my secular attempts at trying to make myself say such things as 'Look at that hot, tight, juicy blank. Wow! I'd like to shove my hot, hard blank up there and blank her good.' I looked at the women and said these kinds of things to myself as fast as I could talk or think. When the naked men with their erections entered the pictures I was excited by them without any attempts to try to make myself think I was. "As I have learned to accept myself, I have realized that being gay is not bad, is not sad, is not something to try to avoid or change. Our only reason, my only reason, for wanting to change in the past has been because of society's disapproval, because I know/knew my friends would not approve of it or accept it, or me and because I had not accepted myself. I am finally learning to accept myself as and for who and what I am. I want to say, I am gay and I am proud. (p. 803, *The Hite Report on Male Sexuality*).

This is becoming the story of many homosexuals who learn the truth about who they are as a person. Since the late nineteenth century the religious leaders have been attempting to cure homosexuality. There have been other therapies used to help them in this matter. Here are thirteen theories to cure homosexuality.

1. PROSTITUTION THERAPY—(late nineteenth century): Through sex with prostitutes, "inverted men" would experience co-gender sexual desire.

2. MARRIAGE THERAPY—(late nineteenth century): When presented with the option of courting and marriage, the "deviant" would naturally go "straight."

3. CAUTERIZATION—(late nineteenth century): Dr. Hammond also suggested that homosexual patients be "cauterized (at) the nape of the neck and lower dorsal and lumbar regions" every ten days.

4. CASTRATION/OVARY REMOVAL—(late nineteenth century): In a pre-Hitler world, the medical community did not consider castration particularly horrific. Aside from believing that removal of the testes would eliminate the sexual drive of the homosexual, many doctors also thought homosexuality to be hereditary.

5. CHASTITY (late nineteenth century): If homosexuality could not be cured, then homosexuals had no moral choice but to remain chaste.

6. HYPNOSIS (late nineteenth/early twentieth century): New Hampshire doctor John D. Quackenbos claimed that "unnatural passions for persons of the same sex"—link nymphomania, masturbation and "gross impurity" could be cured through hypnosis.

7. AVERSION THERAPY (early to mid twentieth century): Reward heterosexual arousal and punish homosexual attraction, often through electric shock.

8. PSYCHOANALYSIS (early to mid twentieth century): With Freud came a whole new discussion of possible cures

through a psychoanalytic approach. In the 1950s, Edmund Berger, M.D., spoke of homosexuality as a kind of "psychic masochism" in which the unconscious sets a person on a course of self-destruction. Find the cause, such as resentment toward a domineering mother, and you find the cure.

9. RADIATION TREATMENT—(early to mid twentieth century): X-ray treatments were believed to reduce levels of promiscuous homosexual urges brought on by glandular hyperactivity.

10. HORMONE THERAPY—(mid twentieth century): If homosexual men are too effeminate and lesbians too masculine, steroid treatments would theoretically butch up the boys and femme out the girls.

11. LOBOTOMY—(mid twentieth century): By cutting serve fibers in the front of the brain, homosexual drives (indeed, most sexual and even emotional reaction capabilities) were eliminated.

12. PSYCHO-RELIGIOUS THERAPY (mid twentieth century): Religious doctors and therapists combined religious teachings with psychoanalysis to inspire heterosexuality.

13. BEAUTY THERAPY (mid twentieth century): All a butch lesbian needs is a good make over. (225, 226, 227, *Reinventing History*).

It seems the radical Christian movement has not progressed with the times. This is not something new. The radical Christian movement is always behind the times and fighting science. The evidence is overwhelming that the vast majority of homosexuals can't change their orientation, no matter what. As we can see over the last couple of centuries, everything under the sun has been tried. Some of the tactics were far fetching. Today we are using gay positive therapy to help homosexuals know who they are as a person. Such therapies used by the radical Christian movement are harmful and have no empirical evidence of their success. Their therapeutic strategies of reinforcing their clients' shame and guilt are professionally unethical.

> Gay Christians are seeking to bring healing to the church, to restore its "peace, unity and purity" by restoring gays and lesbians to the church, and by restoring the church to gays and lesbians. The healing of our sexuality and spirituality may lead to the healing of the sexuality and spirituality of our heterosexual counterparts in the church. Our healing presence may lead the church to a more inclusive community...I believe lesbian and gay Christians are living reminders of the healing that Jesus offered persons of faith. (p. 152, *Homosexuality Opposing Viewpoints*)

The message of gay Christians is Jesus loves you as you are: Jesus Himself never said anything about homosexuality. Today's therapy is to help homosexuals understand who they are and accept themselves as a part of God's creation.

> Some argue that since homosexual behavior is "unnatural," it is contrary to the order of creation. Behind this pronouncement are stereotypic definitions of masculinity and femininity that reflect the rigid gender categories of patriarchal society. There is nothing unnatural about any shared love, even between two of the same gender, if that experience calls both partners into a fuller state of being. Contemporary research is uncovering new facts that are producing a rising conviction that homosexuality, far from being a sickness, sin, perversion or unnatural act, is a healthy, natural and affirming form of human sexuality for some people. Findings indicate that

homosexuality is given fact in the nature of a significant por-
tion of people, and that it is unchangeable. Our prejudice
rejects people or things outside our understanding. But the
God of creation speaks and declares, "I have looked out on
everything I have made and behold it (is) very good." (Gen.
1:31). The word of God in Christ says that we are loved, valued, redeemed and counted as precious no matter how one
might be valued by a prejudiced world. (p. 153, *Homosexuality
Opposing Viewpoints*).

Chapter 8

Homosexuality and Morality

The issue of morality has become the radical Christians' motto. It is amazing they feel they have the edge on morality. In this chapter, we will see their confusion regarding sin and morality. They would have us believe the two concepts (sin and morality) are one and the same. The fact is, sin and morality are two different concepts with different meanings. Coming to a meaning of sin and morality depends on whom you talk with. According to the Bible we see sin as anything that falls short of God's perfection (Romans 3:23). Sin never changes, even though the meaning varies. Morality on the other hand, not only varies in meaning, but also changes over time. For example, a woman at one time would be immoral if she showed her legs in public. This issue has changed with the times. Also cultures change over the years and centuries. Morals are an individual judgement. Again the radical Christians would have us believe they have the edge on morals and they use the Bible as their source. Yet, we cannot forget the Swaggarts and Bakkers who are just a few of many who fail to live by their standards. The radical Christians need to spend more time in their own backyards instead of snooping in their neighbors' backyards. It is hard to define morality in terms of the qualities of good and evil that characterizes human behavior. We cannot measure morality so easily. Defining morality is just as complicated.

Morality, as a global term, refers simply to the relative good-
ness of people as it is reflected in their behavior and beliefs.
Kohlberg (1964) distinguishes between three aspects of
morality; the first two are those to which we are most likely to
react when judging the morals of an individual. There is, to
begin with, the behavioral aspect of morality that is reflected
in a person's ability to resist temptation. Second, there are the
reactions of individuals to their own behavior, specifically to
their transgression of moral rules. Thus, greater morality is
ordinarily associated with greater feelings of guilt following
an immoral act. Individuals who feel little guilt as a result of
immoral behavior are assumed to have lower morals or less
strong consciences than those who feel a great deal of guilt. A
third aspect of morality, and one that is receiving considerable current attention in psychological research, concerns
individual estimates of morality of a given act in terms of
some personal standards of good and evil by which they
judge human behavior. (p. 287, *Adolescents*).

Therefore morality is an individual choice and decision. It is
dependent upon each person's belief system. Morals are standards of
behavior based upon certain values. This happens as each person
assesses the rightness or wrongs of behavior. Society has put some
standards governed by laws, such as thou shall not steal. Some aspects
of morals are easy to define. For example, some issues of sex before
marriage, dancing, drinking and smoking just to name a few are up to
each person's ideals. The radical Christians seek to set into place
morals by interpreting the Bible their way. This is very dangerous for
individual growth and individuality. Each person needs to come to his
or her own understanding of the Bible and morality. For example, the
vast majority of leaders in the radial Christian movement would label
homosexuality as an immoral act. In Sex and Morality they have a
chapter titled "Homosexuality: A Moral Dilemma." They made the following statement:

We called this chapter "Homosexuality: A Moral Dilemma" because it is the only issue we cover where there is considerable doubt whether appropriate and wise choices are available for people who engage in homosexual activity. Whereas heterosexuals may choose to engage in non-marital sex or choose to wait until the right partner comes along for a socially and/or religiously sanctioned marriage, homosexuals cannot choose to wait for a socially and/or religiously sanctioned marriage because there is none at the present time. In this way, their right to choose is denied. As we will see, they did not choose to become homosexuals and they cannot choose to limit their sexual expression to a socially and/or religiously sanctioned relationship. The only way in which they might have the same moral choices as heterosexuals would be for traditional moral belief systems to change so that the homosexual expression of love would be considered as moral as the heterosexual. (p. 167, 168 *Sex and Morality*).

Once again, the radical Christians seek to cap a lid on morality by labeling homosexuality as immoral. Our Western society has been partly shaped by Judeo-Christian thinking. Today this is changing, which has heightened the issue of homosexuality and morality. History did not always share the narrow view presented by the Radical Christian Movement.

The existence of homosexuality since the earliest days of our history is evident from the literature and artifacts of ancient civilizations. Homosexuality has been noted in many cultures throughout the world, and in some it was so acceptable that men who did not engage in homosexual activity may have been considered abnormal. (p. 169, *Sex and Morality*).

This is even true with the Greeks and Romans who accepted homosexuality. Therefore, history's feelings about homosexuality has changed several times throughout history. Therefore, morals are not consistent and change with time. Once again, we must see morals as an individual issue. The sad commentary about homosexuality in the modern world is it's ignorance and stupidity. It is a fact that homosexuals have not had a chance to decide for themselves until recently. The moral dilemma is far from over due to the homophobia that continues. For example, the Miami Herald recently wrote an article titled "Gays enjoying greater tolerance, but moral equality elusive:"

> Recent events paint a pessimistic picture for gay-rights advocates. A United Methodist pastor in Nebraska recently was put on trial by his denomination for performing a wedding-like ceremony for a lesbian couple. In California last month, the state supreme court upheld the right of the Boy Scouts to reject gays. Maine voters have repealed a law that protected gays from discrimination. And state legislatures were flooded with anti-gay legislation last year, with new limits to gay rights proposed in 44 states. Last April, the Florida Legislature adopted the Defense of Marriage Act, barring Florida from recognizing the rights of same-sex marriages performed in other states and forbidding the state from recognizing the rights of same-sex domestic partnerships. Florida and New Hampshire are the only two states in the country that expressly ban adoptions by gays and lesbians. A challenge to that law was snuffed in July when a Broward County judge prevented June Amer, a lesbian Miami-Dade County corrections officer, from adopting a sibling for her young son. Also last year, the Miami-Dade County Commission refused to hear a request for a countywide human rights ordinance preventing discrimination against gays and lesbians. And last month, South Florida leaders of the Presbyterian Church U.S.A. voted down an amendment to church law that would have let local congregations ordain open, sexually active gays. There are several forces propelling the latest wave of anti-gay sentiment. First, there has been a

return to a more conservative values, reflected in part by a falling divorce rate and a drop in out-of-wedlock birth rates (p. 6A The Miami Herald Tuesday, April 21, 1989).

Once again, the radical Christian Movement has sought to define morality and who will have rights. It is sad that society has not broken away from such bigotry and hatred. The fact is that gays and lesbians still do not share the same rights as their heterosexual counterparts. It is time to silence those who seek to deny any group their basic human rights, based upon a misconception of morality. The heterosexual community has denied gays and lesbians their rights because of their own dilemma of high divorce rates and women having children out of wedlock, which is an individual moral issue and cannot be defined by any particular group. It is dangerous and goes against the rights of any individual to make their own moral choices. May freedom soar for all people in the near future.

Chapter 9

Can You Tell?

There are those who say you can tell by looking at a person if they are gay or lesbian. This is another misunderstanding coming out of the radical Christian church. They would have us believe that all gays wear pink panties and high-heels and lesbians wear cowboy boots and pants. In other words, gays are feminine and lesbians are masculine.

"Masculinity and femininity are by no means automatic consequences of being born a boy or girl." (p. 133, *Sex & Behavior*).

There are many factors that come into play with masculinity and femininity of a person. Just like one's orientation is developed at birth. The factors of behavioral, society and genetic have a big part in the development of gender. There are those parents who want to know if they can tell if their child is going to be a homosexual. The answer is no. We cannot predict a child will turn out gay or lesbian based on early childhood behavior or influences, such as tomboy/sissy syndrome.

> Not every tomboy turns out to be a lesbian, nor is every sissy boy growing up gay; even among adults, we all know mannish women and effeminate men who are 100 percent heterosexual. A very feminine little girl may come to prefer females as companions and lovers, and any number of gay men are extremely masculine in manner and appearance. (p. 93, *Now That You Know*).

Even with this fact many gay men are seen as sissies in childhood. For whatever reason, those boys teased in childhood suffer in adulthood. It is the stereotyping of any group that causes psychological/ spiritual ramifications in the future. Those gay men and women who have overcome the bigotry, stereotyping, hatred and lies see their sexual orientation to be an asset rather than a curse. When we begin to look at gender roles we are alluding to the physical aspect of male and female. In society we see the confusion mainly in the masculine and feminine roles.

> Since the masculine and feminine roles are not themselves sharply defined in the same way for all people, and since the relevant qualities of parental behavior are by no means fully recognized by the parents or under their conscious control, there is ample room for variation in the degree to which the abstractly (or ideally) defined gender role will ultimately be performed by the child. Furthermore, we have ample clinical evidence from psychotherapeutic investigations to show that masculinity and femininity are not simply opposite ends of a single dimension, but represent clusters of loosely organized qualities that can vary in strength among themselves. Thus, while the basic definitions of the two roles derive originally from empirical measures of sex differences in behavior, not all the behaviors belonging to the ascribed gender role need to be equally strongly developed. (p. 134, *Sex & Behavior*).

Therefore, we cannot conclude that all effeminate men are gay and all masculine women are lesbians. It is a fact that many gay men are masculine and many lesbians are effeminate.

> Effeminacy is socially defined. It has little to do with the difference between masculinity and femininity. Elements of both are to be found in everyone, once we go beyond the narrowly defined limits of sexual roles. Nor is femininity, whether in homosexuals or heterosexuals, a negative characteristic; it

may well be the most natural expression of an individual's feelings and identity. One person may be more expressive and demonstrative, rulable and excitable, warm and emotional than another. Only when these and other traits are linked together and defined as undesirable do they acquire any value outside of themselves. It may well be that because of our society's negative attitudes toward women and the feminine role, the accusation of effeminacy is used as a criticism directed at some individuals, homosexuals and heterosexuals alike. (p. 70, *The Gay Mystique*)

There have been numerous studies conducted on this issue. Some conclude that the more effeminate males are gay and masculine women are lesbian. More recent research shows that homosexual individuals tend to be androgynous rather than either masculine or feminine. Most gay men can be free to love another man and be more tender, compassionate, supportive, emotional, sensitive and uninhibited. Whereas a straight man is in competition with other men and is uneasy, in most cases, to have such feelings towards women or men. Also, gay men can be free to be tough, stoical and aggressive as a man. In either case they feel free to be either masculine or feminine. Lesbian women can be strong, determined, aggressive and competitive. Also can be delicate, yielding, shy and completely feminine in looks and mannerism. Gays and lesbians make their own mold and do not have to conform to the stereotype of our society. This is being played out in the younger generation of gays and lesbians who have good role models, which the older generations did not have. Most gay men see themselves as men and most lesbian women see themselves as women. Male homosexuals are attracted to other men, not because they see themselves as or wish to be women, but because they are attracted to other men. This attraction is felt for both heterosexuals and homosexuals. This whole masculine and feminine issue has been misunderstood by society, which stems from ignorance, stupidity and homophobia. The key word is homophobia, which fuels the myths about gays and lesbians.

> Homophobia begins in elementary school when "girl," "sissy," "queer," "virgin" and "fag" are the worst putdowns boys can hear. Then, homophobia begins to play itself out in locker-room talk where "the guys" boast of "scoring." To be "cool," and to avoid being called "gay," boys forcibly push for intercourse with girls…Even masturbation is affected by homophobia and misogyny. In the hallways and in sexuality education classes, boys often say, "only fags masturbate" or "why masturbate, you can always find an ugly girl willing to have sex." Homophobia thus encourages boys to label people based on stereotypes to compete with and distance themselves from other boys, and to objectify and even rape girls. (p 29, *Psychological Perspectives on Lesbians and Gay Male Experiences*)

Homophobia affects both heterosexuals and homosexuals. It keeps everyone in a particular role by heightening fears that deviation from traditional gender roles will lead to one being seen as a "fag" or "lezzie." The key is fear, which prevents people from knowing the truth about any given subject. Education is very important in clearing the unknown "fear" about those things we have little knowledge. Understanding gender is a very complex subject.

> Gender development is a complex interaction among biological gender differences; cultural belief systems as expressed both in stereotypes and behaviors and in institutionalized structures such as school and the workplace; and equally important, the child's own developing understanding of gender and what it means to female or male. Gender development originates from the moment of conception. When a female egg unites with a male sperm to form an XX and XY chromosome pair, males and females embark upon different

developmental pathways. The most far-reaching effect of our genetic makeup is determination of physical sexual characteristics. Our physical appearance as male or female has a powerful influence on how we perceive ourselves and are perceived by others, and it is central to the development of gender identity. Also beginning before birth is the production of sex hormones, which do not determine gender development, however. At most, it seems that prenatal sex hormones may facilitate the development of gender role behavior in a male or female direction when postnatal experiences are compatible. (p. 114, *Human Sexuality Opposing Viewpoints*)

There are several factors, which play a part in gender:

1) Parental Influences—This begins at birth. There is no doubt parents have an influence upon their child's gender. Most parents perceive boys to be stronger and rougher than girls, and girls to be more delicate and prettier than boys. Even with parental beliefs and influences with gender, there is a hormone aspect.

2) Hormone—Children by the age of 12 months of age begin to show preferences for sex-typed toys. Each child even though influenced by their parents does have their own temperamental disposition.

It is at this moment that there is an interaction going on between biology and culture, which sets the stage for gender development. It is between the ages of 2 through 5, that children begin to understand for themselves what it means to be male or female. At these ages children already know many of the cultural stereotypes associated with gender. This is not alarming, sense children learn about stereotyping in children's literature, television, parents and teachers.

It is also during the preschool years that gender differences in play begin to emerge more consistently. By age 3, most children greatly prefer to play with same-sex peers when given a choice, and play patterns of female and male groups diverge. We see large differences in toy choice, and parents differential reinforcement of their children's sex-typed toys and activities is strongest at this age. Peers also become important socializing agents, and peers, because they are so gender typed in their beliefs, strongly reinforce gender-typed behaviors. It is almost as if once the child realizes that gender is an important way of categorizing individuals, gender becomes extremely important. (p. 115, *Human Sexuality Opposing Viewpoints*)

Throughout this book we state the fact, that bigotry, hatred and stereotyping of people is not in-born, but learned at an early age. It is not surprising that gender misconceptions about gays and lesbians begins at an early age. These misconceptions about gender roles both homosexual and heterosexual continue throughout one's life, unless they seek to educate themselves on the facts. The issue of gender categorizing has changed and evolved over time. It is important to note that females and males do not differ much in terms of basic cognitive abilities. Also, the patterns of interaction between sexes from birth will follow into adulthood.

3) Biology—The biological make-up of a person is as different as the fingerprints on our hands. Certain groups such as the radical Christian churches fall into error when they fit people into certain groups. For example, all boys are rough and tough. Girls on the other hand are feminine and soft. Yet the biological make-up of people is not always so. In the eyes of some when a person does not fit the so-called norm they are weird, sick, perverted and the list goes on. This is true of homosexuals who have been labeled by the radical Christian churches who seek to control biology. Fact is, none of us can control the biological make-up of humanity. God has made us the unique people we are. Today more than ever we are seeing the stereotyping of gender being reshaped and changed. This is partly due to education, which comes through our technological growth in the past 15 years. Our culture has made some great advances in the area of gender conforming.

Given the evidence that gender differences are at least partly biologically based, is it the case that these differences are inevitable? We think not. First, although there are slight biological differences between infant males and females, it is certainly true that these differences can be exaggerated or diminished by the prevailing cultural beliefs. That is, cultures determine which aspects of behavior will be deemed important, and through socialization and institutional structures, will communicate to each developing member of the culture the appropriate norms of behavior. Second, we are already seeing many changes in gender-related behaviors, especially since the early 1970s. More women are entering the work force, and more women are entering traditionally male jobs. Family structures are changing as well. Families today encompass a much broader range of relationships and roles than the more traditional families of the past. (p. 118, 119 *Human Sexuality Opposing Viewpoint*).

Such changes are important in the scope of things. It will allow the whole concept of female and male roles to evolve and get away from stereotypes.

The finding that gender differences in psychopathology among homosexuals are similar to those of heterosexuals may provide an evidence against the gender role reversal hypothesis. For example, gender differences in anxiety and phobic disorders among homosexual and heterosexual groups tend to show similar trends. It appears that except for their sexual orientation, homosexual and heterosexual individuals are not significantly different in psychological adjustment and behavior. (p. 165, *Male and Female Homosexuality*).

Chapter 10

Coming Out

Coming-out is a process, which most gays and lesbians go through. Once they accept the feelings which have been buried deep within the subconscious, because of society's reactions to homosexuality in the past, forces the gay and lesbian to deny their true self. When a gay or lesbian discovers himself or herself to be homosexual they are faced with many options.

Until very recently, there were few fulfilling options for a man who discovered himself to be homosexual. He could pretend that he was heterosexual—perhaps even marry and have children—and either (a) spend his life tormented by suppressed feelings and by the knowledge that he was living a lie or (b) lead a clandestine second life, sneaking off to one-night stands with other men, married or unmarried, who also were leading clandestine second lives. There was a third possibility: falling in love with a man and making a home with him. Though laws and social conventions made this a difficult, even dangerous proposition, some managed to carry it off anyway. But they lived on tenterhooks; they were as secretive about their private lives as enemy spies; they risked losing everything—job, home social position, even freedom—if someone who didn't like their homosexuality decided to make an issue of it and exposed them. (p. 32 A Place at the Table).

The options have been limited until the Gay Liberation of the 1970s, which has helped gays and lesbians. Coming-out still can have grave consequences. Homophobia still remains an enduring form of prejudice, but we have made some progress since the 1970s. As more gays and lesbians come out of the closet society will begin to know the facts about homosexuality. Those still in the closet, which some are married, face an uncertain future. The fear of coming out is great. Also the emotions and feelings that have been buried for so long run wild. This is one man's story:

> Throughout his childhood, from age five on, Derek would sneak off with a friend into someone's basement or the woods along the back alley, where they would take off their pants and play with each other, usually fondling each others genitals. It became habitual. "At that time, I didn't quite have a name for it," says Derek, "It was something that I liked doing, that felt good, that I wanted to do as often as I could. The other kids recognized it as being something bad and dirty. And all I wanted to know was, When can we do it again?" By the time he was fourteen, he began to put two and two together. Something clicked. Although he only had a murky sense of what it meant to be "gay," the label seemed to fit him. "I was just thinking it through, analyzing the situation to death, asking myself, What does this mean? And I realized I might be gay," Derek says. "Once identifying that, I came to the conclusion that these were the cards I was dealt. I knew people didn't approve of it, so I decided to keep it to myself rather than open myself up to ridicule." (p. 4, *Passages of Pride*)

The fear of being ridiculed is the mental anguish most gays and lesbians face in the beginning stages of coming-out. There is no certain way, or process, of coming out of the closet. Each person's story is somewhat the same, but the stages can vary. Also the coming-out process depends on each person's given situation; such as family, friends and other support systems. Whatever the situation, the coming-out process is filled with lots of emotions. At the basis of the coming-out is bigotry and hatred. This alone can cause the fear to heighten. Unless they can overcome this fear, the closet doors stays shut. The closed door brings about psychological and spiritual pain. Once again, Derek's story makes this point clear:

> At Highland Park, Derek's teachers uttered hardly a word about homosexuality, except for the harsh accusation that it was homosexuals who got AIDS. Early in the year, at the beginning of a swimming lesson, a gym teacher delivered a stern warning to his class: "If you find anyone looking at you, let me know and I'll get him out of here." Another teacher condemned gays and lesbians as "perverts who have no purpose or place in a civilized society," Derek recalls. Though they were unaware of it, these role models—teachers and coaches that he respected and looked to for guidance and approval—were negating a fundamental piece of Derek's personality. The dubious messages made him even more introverted, and pushed him deeper into the closet. Not for an instant did he consider disclosing his sexual orientation. (p. 8, *Passages of Pride*).

Those who have come out of the closet as a gay or lesbian, did not do so over night. There are many obstacles to overcome. It is those with a strong will to fight those obstacles, that bring about healing. These are just some of the obstacles that gays and lesbians face in coming-out:

1. Acceptance—No matter what some people may think, a gay person must accept who they are. This may require counseling. Heterosexual parents with the values of the heterosexual majority

raised most gays and lesbians. They are expected to marry and have children. But when they realize their attraction and feelings for someone of the same gender is ok, it changes their course. Being able to say I am normal and accept who I am is a big step.

2. Dealing with the emotions—Because the feelings have been buried deep within the subconscious, gays and lesbians must sort out these feelings. When gays and lesbians finally get in touch with these feelings they are able to correct their feelings.

3. Mend the hurt—Over time being ridiculed, hated, condemned and lied about causes much pain. Through counseling and support gay people are able to begin the process of taking off the layers of hurt. Being able to forgive and understand homophobics is important in the mending.

4. Know yourself—Gaining a strong understanding of who we are as a gay or lesbian will help us withstand the bigotry. When we know ourselves we can then sort out the garbage of society. It does not control us, but we control it.

5. Out of the Closet—In building a good foundation of who, what, where, when and why of our being, then we can step out into the light. When a gay person does come out of the closet they have begun to count the cost. They will no longer hide their feelings and emotions. In coming-out they are saying to the world, "I am proud of who I am." Support and love from friends or loved ones helps in this decision.

Until gays and lesbians are totally free to be who they are, they will continue to struggle with certain aspects of coming-out. The process is sometimes a life-long process. Some gays feel a sense of loss when coming out of the closet. Other's coming-out is an exciting experience. A therapist gives us a conclusion of lesbians coming-out:

> Clients of mine who have grieved either during the coming-out process or at a later date, have responded with great relief at feeling permission to express feelings they had often felt were unacceptable or politically incorrect. One woman

responded with tears when I asked if there were anything she would miss of her heterosexual lifestyle. She said she felt sad that she would never have the family approval her brother had because he was married. She also said that it felt good to finally cry about not going to her high school prom. She had felt like such a failure for not having a date even though she knew that she was not attracted to men. Clients also have expressed that, after grieving, they are much less angry with their families and straight friends. (p. 220, *Gays and Lesbian Mental Health*)

Coming-out takes a lot of energy and time. Again, the coming-out process varies. The dynamics can be overwhelming, as we have shown. What is the peak of coming-out? This is a good question. Usually that occurs when a gay person comes out to family and friends. Once they do this they are able to deal with the rest.

Coming out to family is considered a significant event in lesbian/ gay identity development, from both a personal and political perspective. Not being out to one's family is often linked to an early stage of identity development. Pressures come from internal sources (i.e., "I should be out to the ones I love,") and from external sources ("You're not helping your community [gay] if you're not out completely."). For some, the fear of coming out may indeed be a developmental issue. (p. 146, *Gay and Lesbian Mental Health*)

In coming-out we see the issues at hand, but greater than that is how gays and lesbians go through the process. As we look at the process there is a lot of content. How one approaches the issues is the key point. It is easy to talk about how gays and lesbians come out of the closet. It is critical for gays, lesbians, family, friends and counselors to take one step at a time. Most of all gays and lesbians do not need to come out alone. Having a strong support system makes the process a lot easier. One thing we can see out of this chapter is the importance of gays and lesbians coming-out of the closet and into the light. Just like flowers cannot grow under a rock, nor can gays and lesbians blossom and be the wonderful people they are by hiding in the closet.

Chapter 11

The Family

The radical Christian movement screams from the rooftops that homosexuals are out to destroy the family. They speak from their pulpits that homosexuals will make their children homosexuals. Also they are out to destroy the concept of family. It seems they feel they have the true understanding of family. In this chapter, we will look at the misconceptions coming out of the radical Christian movement regarding homosexual families. We will look at the concept of family through the centuries. Most of all, this chapter will show the results of the radical Christian's goal to proclaim homosexuals as unfit parents. To prove our point, William Norman Grigg makes the following statement:

> Every society that has accepted homosexuality as normal has suffered as a result, William Norman Grigg maintains in the following viewpoint. Examining several cultures of ancient and medieval Europe, Grigg argues that homosexuality invariably disrupted the family, promoted pedophilia and child slavery, and contributed to the moral decline of society. Grigg warns that America's increasing tolerance toward the homosexual lifestyle will lead to the destruction of the family. Grigg is the author of The Gospel of Revolt: Feminism Versus Family Values. (p. 79, *Human Sexuality Opposing Viewpoints*)

This viewpoint is an extreme understanding of homosexuals and family. The problem with misconceived ideas about homosexuality leads to extreme viewpoints, which hurts a lot of people. The radical Christian movement has a misunderstanding of the term family. The makeup of family in society is very diverse, which makes it impossible for a group like the radical Christian movement to sew a "one size fits all." Yet, the radical Christian holds up as a norm the Cleaver type family. Where the father works and the wife stays home as a homemaker. The radical Christian movement sees the family where the husband is authoritative and the wife is submissive. This group would have the world believe homosexual practice is essentially anti-family and undermines human sexuality. This view shows the radical Christian's narrowness of human sexuality. Procreation is just a segment to human sexuality. Their thinking has a big effect upon the homosexual community. For example, homosexuals have a hard time adopting children, keeping their own children (when they come out of the closet) and being truthful about their orientation. This no doubt causes psychological and spiritual chaos in homosexuals. The traditional viewpoint of a mother, father and two children is not even Biblical. In the Bible a family was noted to be a tribe of people. Families could be a father, mother, aunt, uncle, grandparents and children. The people of Israel were called a family. The Bible gives us a different picture of family:

> Moses was reared by a foster parent, the Pharaoh's daughter. Scholars agree that Joseph was much older than Mary, so much of Jesus' life could have been spent in a single-parent family. The apostle Paul's young protege, Timothy, was the product of an inter-generation family—a loving mother and grandmother. The home Jesus spent much time in during his ministry was made up of three adult siblings living as family—Mary, Martha and Lazarus. The pivotal leader of the church in Philippi was Lydia, who was head of a large household and a businesswoman. (p. 34, *National Forum*)

Even with the facts, the radical Christian movement continues to tell the world that homosexuals are unfit parents. They conclude that they can't reproduce (therefore recruit), deviant in its form and psychologically ill. It is their continued thinking that causes the following:

> The rise in hostility toward gay parents has corresponded directly to their increased visibility, the result of bitter public disputes over child custody and foster placement policies. (p. 95, *After the Ball*)

Can you imagine the psychological turmoil a gay and lesbian must go through to prove their worth? There are many gays and lesbians raising children and doing a good job. In one of our earlier chapters we noted both U.C.L.A psychiatrists Martha Kirkpatrick and Richard Green, a psychiatrist at the State University of New York Stoney Brook studied children being raised by homosexual parents. They could not find any signs of confused sexual identity in the children. There were no signs of emotional disturbances or sexual identity as the radical Christian movement would have the world to believe. Dr. Harold M. Voth, in his book titled: *Families The Future of America*, gives us the ideal thinking of homophobia, which states the fall of the family is due to the sick, grossly deviant and maladjusted people. (p. 32-33) He makes his thoughts clear about homosexuals:

> Our national public health policy should include a posture on homosexuality along with other illnesses which have vast social implications. Such a public policy would stimulate the creation of both private and public treatment centers. To weave homosexuality into the fabric of society by "normalizing" the condition is destructive to both the individual and society. (p. 173 *Families The Future of America*)

It is this attitude, which causes psychological and mental torture to any such group. This misguided thinking is nothing more than bigotry, hatred and lies in full swing. Such professionals show their

ignorance and stupidity. Their lack of knowledge on the subject produces fear. They say that children raised by gay parents will bring up
confused little children. Once again, the facts do not support such
thinking:

> This fear is apparently groundless. In February 1988, the New
> York Times summarized a recent professional report on gay-
> parented households; based on the results of seventeen sepa-
> rate clinical studies, the report found "nothing unusual in
> gender identity development, no greater preference for
> homosexuality, and no serious social and emotional malad-
> justment" among the children of gay parents. (p. 96, *After The
> Ball*)

It is time to silence the ignorance and stupidity. It is this type of
thinking which brings Hitlers into power. Just like Hitler, the radical
Christian movement blames the illnesses of society upon homosexuals, just like Hitler used Jews and homosexuals.

> The persecution and attempted extermination of homosexu-
> als represents but one part of the exhaustive crusade the
> Nazis launched to purge Germany of contragenics of all
> kinds and to create an Aryan elite that would dominate
> Europe and, finally, the world…A number of historians have
> interpreted the Nazis' war as a crusade, kindled not by greed
> for territorial and material gains but by a mission: to create an
> exclusively Aryan utopia. (p. 182, *The Pink Triangle*)

Hitler sought to blame those groups he hated in order to annihilate
them off the earth. It is these tactics the radical Christian movement
uses in subtle, but Christian ways. They truly believe the world would
be a utopia, if it were totally Christian. Therefore their mission is to
silence any group, which fails to follow their rule of thinking. It is
common knowledge that homosexuality is the subject of continuing
and long-standing hostility of the radical Christian movement. There

are several specific sources of anti-homosexual prejudice, which have a direct implication towards the family. First, there is the view that homosexuality is "unnatural" because it does not involve heterosexual reproduction. Yet, Dr. Judd Marmor in his book titled: "Homosexual Behavior: A Modern Reappraisal" makes the following statement:

> Homosexuality is far from being "unnatural" in the statistical sense. It occurs in all higher species, even when members of the opposite sex are present and available for mating. (p. 26, *Homosexual Behavior: A Mod Reappraisal*)

Secondly, there is the view that Homosexuals are a threat to children, which does not hold up to the facts stated earlier:

> This notion persists despite well-documented evidence that it is false (Burgess et al., 1978; De-Francis, 1966; Groth & Birnbaum, 1978; Kffempe & Kemp, 1984). Fear for the safety of children, unfortunately, is a source of strong, irrational reaction on the part of the public. The notion that homosexuality is incompatible with children or child rearing may contribute to the image of homosexuals as "family-less." (p. 12, *Homosexuality and Family Relations*)

These are just several of many views which the radical Christian movement uses in order to make its case against homosexual families. Whatever the case may be it does not support the facts given about homosexuals and their families. It is their homophobia, which is the issue. Homophobia is a social disease that needs to be eliminated.

We know that gays and lesbians have been a part of documented-recorded history, and have not always had a negative aspect. It is a known fact that homosexuality was acceptable in ancient Greece among adolescent males until completion of their military training. Homosexuality has not been accepted in the Judeo-Christian Era. In the Judeo-Christian thinking family is tied into procreation, which comes out of the book of Genesis. The story of Adam and Eve is their

REV. JERRY STEPHENSON, Th.D., Ph.D.   107

basis. We have come a long way since then, to the Cleavers and the Brady Bunch. Our Western thinking of family does not fit ancient history. Procreation is not the only function of the family. There is no doubt that procreation is important for the family line to continue. Family is more than having children:

> One of the main functions of the family is for it to be a "haven in a heartless world" (Lasch, 1977). It is within the supportive milieu of the family where all members are to be loved nurtured so that healthy growth and development occurs. (p. 1, *Homosexuality and Family Relations*)

A family is a place where one finds security, love and support. By looking at the American so-called family, we see its failure to be a haven of rest in a cruel world. Maybe the American family might learn something from homosexual families. This has not happened yet, because of the societal stigma which does not associate homosexuals as part of a family unit, which they were born into and later develop on their own (lover and children). In looking at the growing information on the psychological development of gays and lesbians and their natural families, one is sure to ask why gays and lesbians identities are troubling to them and their families. This is, no doubt, due to the societal stigma. This not only affects gays and lesbians, but their family. It causes a disturbance in what society and religion calls, "the family unit."

> The existing literature, however, suggests a commonality of issues and themes in both individual homosexual identity development and family member adjustment to having a homosexual relative. This similarity of issues suggests that a profitable theoretical and practical synthesis of our understanding of personal family adjustment is possible. This synthesis is rooted in societal definitions of deviance and their effects on personal and familial identity. In the present paper, I will sketch out a framework for understanding the

psychological adjustment of both homosexual family members and their relatives. This frame work is developed on the basic assertion that the nature of family reaction, and its long-term effects, are both understandable and coherent when viewed as the product of having a major social deviance uncovered within the close environment of the family circle (p. 10, *Homosexuality. and Family Relations*)

Education is the key. The process to understanding something that society and religion has rejected will take time. In a sense, there must be a deprogramming of information. There will be a creation of a positive identity for their gay loved-one and the family members. This is just the beginning to understanding the concept of family. Unfortunately, there are those professionals which seem to have a strong religious belief, that still treat homosexuality as a mental illness. The religious validation of anti-homosexual prejudice reinforces the basic view of gays and lesbians as undesirable and deviant persons in society and the family. This type of thinking stems from homophobia, which clouds the truth. Homophobia is basically the fear of something, in this case, it is the unknown aspects of gays and lesbians. This can stem from ignorance or stupidity. In either case we know that homophobia has a negative effect. Peter J. Gomes, an American Baptist minister and professor of Christian morals at Harvard University sums up this chapter best by explaining homophobia:

As "the last respectable prejudice of the century." Certainly there is no other prejudice in which people feel more morally justified; no other prejudice that reaches so high into the ranks of the intelligent, the powerful, the otherwise quite virtuous; no other prejudice, therefore, more deep-seated and polarizing. There is, one would wager, no other prejudice that takes more irrational forms. One sees Christians hatefully reviling homosexual love in the name of Christ, whose supreme commandment was to "love one another." And one sees defenders of "the family" citing gay rights as the greatest threat to "family values"—as if anything that deserved the name of "family values" didn't include the idea of parents responding humanely to the news of their child's homosexuality, as if it somehow served the cause of "the family" to heap abuse on the idea of same-sex couples (the obvious alternative, to which, of course, to gay promiscuity). (p. 82, *A Place At The Table*)

The concept of family goes beyond the Judeo-Christian thinking. Even in the Old Testament the concept of family could be a nation, blood relatives or religious beliefs. The whole concept of gays and lesbians still grips certain people, especially the radical Christian churches. Add the concept of homosexual families and you get total chaos. This attitude causes the oppression of gays and lesbians to live.

To illustrate, the United States Supreme Court recently upheld the constitutionality of a Georgia law maintaining that the right to privacy does not extend to homosexual activity. Police harassment of homosexuals in gay settings such as bars is commonplace. Homosexuals may not marry one another and because of this are denied social security and insurance benefits, inheritance rights, and major medical benefits for live-in lovers. Gays are barred from military service. Some states ban gay adoptions and, in some, home ownership by unrelated individuals is illegal. (p. 2, *Homosexuality and Family Relations*)

No wonder gays and lesbians suffer from an identity crisis. That such oppression and lack of freedom causes psychological, social, mental and spiritual pain. Again, until gays and lesbians are able to come out of the closet and have the same basic rights as heterosexuals they will continue to face difficulties. It is time to end the ignorance, stupidity, bigotry and lies about gays and lesbians. Only once society overcomes its homophobia and understands homosexuality, will total healing come to gays, lesbians, their friends and families.

Chapter 12

Narcissism and Homosexuality

Where does narcissism fit in with the subject of homosexuality? This is the question we will answer in this chapter. Before we can answer this question, we need to understand the concept. The American Heritage Dictionary states it this way:

> 1. Excessive admiration of oneself. 2. Psychoanalysis an arresting of development at, or regression to, the infantile stage of development in which one's own body is the object of erotic interest. (p. 872, *The American Heritage Dictionary*)

It is of no surprise that many homosexuals feel shame, guilt and depression due to radical Christian views of homosexuality as sick and a sin. When any group is suppressed, such as homosexuals, it is going to cause some problems. What it has done in the past is keep the homosexual in the closet. It is the masking of their feelings to others, often exaggerating the opposite feelings in interpersonal relations. This use of narcissistic defense has caused the view that there is a higher incidence of narcissism in homosexuals than in heterosexuals. The problem with the term "narcissism", is when it was borrowed from Freud:

The term narcissism was borrowed by Freud from Havelock Ellis, who used the Greek name to describe a form of sexual perversion in which the individual takes himself as a sexual object. (p. 2, *Gay & Lesbian Mental Health*)

Since Freud's viewpoint, narcissism has taken on other understandings as an "inflated false self." The term narcissism comes from the Greek myth, superficially understood to represent self-love. It is noted that narcissism is a natural process. There are professionals who go so far as to say that a normal and healthy case of narcissism is important to a healthy adaptation. Therefore, the shame that groups such as homosexuals deal with causes the fear of being found out.

Defenses are employed to protect against narcissistic vulnerability and exposure, and by default, the development of a healthy sense of self is hindered. We can clearly see how much of the above could account for narcissistic traits in gay men, but the question remains as to whether there really is a connection between male homosexuality and narcissism. Presently, narcissism is assessed by way of clinical interview and psychological testing, and psychological testing has frequently been used to study the personality structure of male homosexuals. (p. 5, *Gay & Lesbian Mental Health*)

The study of homosexuality by way of psychological testing is not new. The Minnesota Multiphasic Personality Inventory (MMPPI) was noted to be the most used test on homosexuals. The results of the test were noted by Hooker (1972):

"Found that blind judges could not distinguish homosexual men's responses on projective tests from those of heterosexual men." (p. 5, *Gay & Lesbian Mental Health*) From this, we realize there is no difference from each group's psychodynamic conflicts. Another test used is the Rorschach Inkblot Test.

Most of the studies that were published using the Rorschach implemented hospitalized patients. Also, other tests used prisoners. Dr.

Alexander and his colleagues wanted to assess whether a group of psychologically healthy gay men would give clearer results to the Rorschach. Included in the study was the Narcissistic Personality Inventory, which is a 40 item self-report measure designed to measure individual differences in narcissism as a personality trait. Being able to submit a representative sample in any group is not easy, because each person is somewhat different in nature.

> What the results do indicate, however, is that our sample did produce a statistically greater likelihood of offering a Reflection response to the Rorschach, with five of the 32 subjects offering at least one. Interestingly, however, the subjects in this study had a mean NPI score of 14.43. Thus our sample scored below the mean (which is 16.50) on this measure. When compared to those subjects who were rejected from this study, our sample had a statistically higher MMPI EgoStrength score (a measure of self-esteem). Other findings revealed that of the subjects we assessed 31 percent scored positive on the Rorschach Depression Constellation. Further, our sample scored above the expected mean on Rorschach measures of introspection, oppositionality, and emotional control. (p. 8, *Gay & Lesbian Mental Health*)

What we can see from the study is the complexity of homosexual personality structure. These tests cannot explain a trait such as narcissism. It will take other studies to begin to understand the human component. We cannot forget the oppression, bigotry and hatred many homosexuals must overcome at the hands of the radical Christian movement. When will the radical Christian movement admit to their homophobia, which suppresses such groups as homosexuals. For example, for hundreds of years the radical Christian movement, along with other bigots convinced the world that blacks could not learn like whites. The issue at hand was that blacks were not allowed the same opportunity as whites to get a valued education. It is this type of suppression which allows the radical Christian movement to put their blame on such issues as narcissism. This chapter has sought to show that narcissism is in all walks of life. It is also a natural process in normal people. Therefore, we conclude with a statement made by Dr. Christopher J. Alexander:

> Societal homophobia, selective acceptance, and the necessity, on the part of the homosexual, to size up an individual or situation before letting down one's guard all contribute to a hypersensitivity of one's role vis-a-vis others. Confronted with circumstances such as these, one can argue that the self-focus used by homosexual men is not to affirm a sense of grandiosity and entitlement, nor is the need of tribute from others (Kernberg, 1975) about self-idealization. Rather, a focus on the self may be adaptive as the individual looks within to formulate his own view of self, compared to what he senses from others. That guilt and shame are major components of the person who feels inferior and inadequate are themes we often see in clients. Thus, perhaps the etiology of this familiar struggle is, as Lewis (1987) points out, consistent with what psychoanalysts have long believed: that being in a chronic state of guilt is a defense against forbidden grandiosity or narcissism. Further, the need for recognition from others is likely a very primal desire for affirmation and acceptance, rather than some attempt to have others collude in one's feelings of greatness. (p. 10, *Gay & Lesbian Mental Health*)

Chapter 13

Homosexuality Is a Choice

The radical Christian movement would have the world believe that homosexuality is a choice one makes. Can you imagine a person wanting to become a homosexual. Yes, become a homosexual. Be denied a job and housing. You can be kicked out of the military, if they find out you are homosexual. Yes, be condemned by the church as an abomination and going to hell. Come out of the closet and be bashed by a bigot. These are some of the things homosexuals face when they let the world know they are homosexuals. These are not the qualities that would cause one to want to be a homosexual. The opposite is going to happen. Those homosexuals who realize who they are overcome such issues as stated above. Just like any human behavior, sexual orientation and sexual identity are multi-determined. They are not something you choose, but a matter of discovery. During a person's early years they slowly become aware of what their sex is, and what sex they are attracted to. A person does not just sit down, think things over, and then logically "decide" to be what they are. Rather, a person becomes aware of what motives nature and their environment have given them.

> Sexual orientation appears to be determined prior to adolescence and prior to homosexual or heterosexual activity. The most important single predictor of adult homosexuality was a self-report of homosexual feelings, which usually occurred

three years before genital homosexual activity. (p. 169, *Psychology The Science of Behavior "White Book"*)

It needs to be noted that a person's sexual orientation (homosexual, heterosexual, bisexual) is determined by one or more of the following factors: genetic, hormonal, psychological or social. One's orientation depends upon the individual person. One must answer the following question. How does one have a choice to be a homosexual? The fact is that most homosexuals grew up in a heterosexual world, had heterosexual parents, went to heterosexual schools and lived in a heterosexual society. That does not leave any room for choice. It is a noted fact that most homosexuals have tried to change their orientation because of society's view on homosexuality. Therefore, the radical Christians' view of choice gives way to change. A homosexual cannot change who they are no more than a person with blue eyes. Just as heterosexuals do not change or choose their feelings of sexual attraction, gay and lesbians don't choose theirs. The real choices are between suppressing these feelings of same-sex attraction or pretend to be asexual or heterosexual. Homosexuals can't change, and to try is unrealistic and harmful.

To pray for a change in sexual orientation is about as meaningful as to pray for a change from blue eyes to brown. Furthermore, there is no healthy way to reverse or change sexual orientation once it is established. The claim of certain groups to be able to change homosexuals into heterosexuals has been shown to be spurious and frequently based on homophobia (cf. Ralph Blair's pamphlet "Ex-Gay" (HCCC Inc., 1982). The usual technique used to bring about this pseudo-change involves helping gay persons internalize self-hatred, an approach that frequently causes great psychological harm and suffering. The Christian communities that make use of this sort of ministry usually do so to avoid any challenge to their traditional attitude and to avoid any dialogue with self-accepting gays and truly professional psychotherapists. (p. 30)

For many years the Ex-Gay Movement encouraged change, but in present years due to studies of homosexuality showing a genetic link they embrace a new philosophy: "Yes, they are homosexual," but, like the alcoholic cannot touch another drink, nor can a homosexual touch another man. Therefore, they once again see homosexuality as a disease. We have proven earlier, that homosexuality is not a disease or mental illness. The foundation of the Ex-Gay Movement is the Bible. Therefore, change is based upon Scripture and not science. The sad commentary is that many Ex-Gay's struggle with homosexuality throughout their lives. Many end up slipping back into homosexuality, which will be proven by a report within this chapter. Not only is the Ex-Gay hurt psychologically, mentally, and spiritually, but so are their families (wife and children). One example:

8 July 1992

Dear Rev. Stephenson,

After reading the interview article about you which appeared in the Metro Section of the Sun Sentinel on Monday, July 6, 1992, I feel that I need to write to you. I am sure that I am not alone when I say 'BOY, HAVE I GOT A STORY TO TELL YOU!' We are quite alike, you and I, and I believe that you may benefit from my story and possibly be interested in talking after you have read it.

Just the facts…I came from a conservative Christian Mid-West family who decided that my emerging homosexuality was not acceptable. At the suggestion of my local pastor and with the approval of my parents, I moved away from home and attended the Quest Learning Center in Reading, PA, for nearly two years in the mid-1980's. I counseled personally with Mr. Colin Cook, Quest's founder, and co-founder of Homosexuals Anonymous.

Based on your experience, I am sure that you are familiar with both of these 'change' organizations. However, I shall briefly elaborate on what they are. Quest Learning Center was a counseling center— change ministry—supported by the Adventist Church. The program consisted of a weekly private therapy session, weekly growth class, and weekly H.A. meeting. H.A., of course, is a 14-step program similar to A.A. but designed to help persons 'live in freedom from homosexuality'.

At the time I moved to Reading, I was 20 years old and relatively naive—never having been in a gay bar and had only VERY limited gay sexual experiences (I could count them on one hand). In fact, I had not even begun to 'come out' when my parents approached me about visible 'changes' and demanded that I 'get this resolved'. Within the first two weeks of arriving in Reading, I found a nice studio apartment, landed a good job, and had slept with another counselee twice—once in Colin Cook's bed while he and his wife were away on a speaking engagement.

To make a long story short, while at Quest, I met my first and (to date) only lover—another counselee, Craig. Craig and I were together for over 18 months and were very much in love. Needless to say, I was subject to increasing pressure from Colin to end the relationship while Craig grew increasingly sure that there was no 'cure'. The polarity of the situation nearly created schizophrenia in me, as I could not seem to choose one over the other. Eventually, the relationship deteriorated and a series of events lead to its painful and bitter demise. I left Craig and Quest and moved to Florida almost 8 years ago. Then, things became REALLY difficult.

It took me nearly four years to get over the relationship and separate myself from the Quest experience. For a long time while I was at Quest and after, I believed that it could work—that I could be cured.

I followed many of the same paths you did in the search for healing and heterosexuality. The latter never came. Since then, I have reconciled my Christianity and my homosexuality and feel very comfortable in both. This has come after years of thinking, years of praying, years of learning who and what I am, and years of painful and difficult growth.

After I moved to Florida, I was instrumental in founding "Worthy Creations Ministry"—a local change ministry associated with a Baptist church on Davie Boulevard and assisted in founding a local chapter of H.A. I conducted meetings, appeared on TBN, radio, and in several newspapers all in support of the 'change' theology. With my assistance, W.C.M. incorporated, received tax-exempt nonprofit status, and set up and financed a residence apartment in Fort Lauderdale for AIDS victims that remains operational to date. I also conducted seminars locally and in Orlando and even authored a seminar that was to have been presented at a national convention of 'change ministries' in California.

However, I resigned from the ministry because I could no longer proclaim 'freedom from homosexuality' when underneath, I wanted many of the men I sought to assist. Additionally, the autocratic director of the ministry and I had different visions of the ministry and I could not bear the constant conflict. Since my resignation, I have not been involved in any pro-gay religious organizations partially because of my formal local involvement and partially because I have since resolved my inner conflicts and found peace.

After my departure from Quest many years ago, an Adventist pro-gay group called Kinship presented a research paper to the church hierarchy in which the stories of 17 counselees were told. All of the counselees had been molested or sexually approached by Quest's 'cured' director, Colin Cook. It was a tremendous local scandal.

Craig was instrumental in assisting Kinship to find the persons to interview as both Craig and I knew several men who were sexually intimate with Colin during the time I was there. Quest was closed and the funding pulled. Colin publicly apologized and was placed in a church-dictated counseling program. H.A. continues to operate, though it was seriously damaged by the scandal. Last month, Colin, who was not licensed or who had no formal psychological credentials, and his family moved to Colorado where restrictions on counselors are the least of any state in the U.S.

I am very familiar with the literature and theology of both sides to this issue—possessing numerous volumes, books, pamphlets, and other materials published in this regard. I have personally met many of the top writers and theologians on this issue through my contacts in the 'change ministry' arena. Similarly, I have many contacts in the pro-gay Christian movement.

Why then have I remained hidden? Why have I not spoken out? These are difficult questions for which I have no definitive answers at present. I can say that I am in the process of writing a screenplay about Quest and my experiences there. Perhaps, this is the way I shall speak out—for now, at least.

Now, you know the basics of my story. Naturally, it is far more complex and intricate than I have described here. I would guess that I am lucky to have gone through it and learned to be who and what I am—a gay Christian—and live in comfort with both. God has richly blessed me thorough this and I continue to pray that one day, He will give me a partner of similar calling and similar wholeness.

Thank you for listening. I am sorry to have been so verbose, but I felt that you might benefit from reading my story. Surely, there are others who might take courage and strength from it. Naturally, I thank you for your confidentiality and discretion in this matter as I have disclosed this story to only a few persons.

If there is anything I can do or if you desire to talk more about this, lease feel free to contact me at my office during business hours at

_____. I will be happy to set aside some time to meet with you if you would be so inclined.

God richly bless you and your work, Jerry (and Rex).

Sincerely in Him,

_____

This is just one of many such stories of Ex-gays who tried to change and finally realized who they were as a homosexual shows the psychological, mental, and spiritual roller coaster they must endure. The story about the Ex-Gay minister who told the world he longer struggled with homosexuality is not uncommon. This is the story with so many gay Christians. The truth is that most, if not all, Ex-gays struggle with homosexuality. Yet, I have never heard of a heterosexual struggling with homosexuality. These Ex-gay groups go some-thing like this: "They come together and sit in a circle. The group opens up with prayer and sings a few songs. Someone in the group will share their success story. Then group then breaks up into groups of females in one group and males in another group. In these groups they share their struggles. It is always the same story with a sad ending. Those who say they overcome are like our story above. They tell the world they do not struggle anymore, but behind close doors the truth is known. Many end up leaving the Ex-Gay groups and church. They spend years believing they are living in sin and God does not love them. Thank God for those gay Christians who know different. Gay

Christians come to the realization that God loves them for who they are. They bring hope to the Ex-Gay movement. No longer do homosexuals need to feel condemned by God, nor do they need to live in the closet. The closet is the worst place for anyone to be. The radical Christian movement seeks to keep homosexuals in the closet. As we enter the next millennium hopefully the closet doors will be torn down.

Homosexuality is no more a choice than heterosexuality. The exact causes of heterosexuality and homosexuality are unknown. The results of sexual orientation are likely to be the results of several different factors, including genetic, hormonal and environmental factors. Biological (genetic, hormonal, neurological) have a strong case. For example, Bailey and his co-author, Dr. Richard Pillard, a psychiatry professor at Boston University School of Medicine conducted a study of twins. The results of the study gave clues to homosexuality. "California researches reported in Late August that a cluster of brain cells that might guide men's sex drive is twice as large in heterosexual males as in homosexual males." (p. 17A Miami Herald) There have been other studies of the brain done by Dr. Laura Allen and Dr. Roger Gorski of the University of California at Los Angeles. This report follows Dr. Simon LeVay of the Salk Institute in LaJolla California who makes the following statement:

> A region of the hypothalamus, a part of the brain that helps regulate sexual behavior, was smaller in homosexual men than in heterosexual men; it was equivalent to the dimensions seen in heterosexual women. (p. 8A Miami Herald)

Dr. Simon LeVay praised Dr. Laura Allen and Dr. Roger Gorski's report. He stated it was correct and showed clear results, and in a way it's more important than his own findings. There was also a study showing brain difference in gay males conducted by Dr. Martin Reite, professor of psychiatry at the University of Colorado Health Sciences center. The discoveries of brain difference varied in each study, but do point to a strong case of brain differences between homosexual males and heterosexual males. With all these studies, the radical Christian movement would have us believe that no research has been done to prove a genetic link. There have been more studies to prove a genetic link than studies to show no genetic link. To the radical Christian movement homosexuality is a sin, a willful choice of godless evil. To many orthodox behaviorists, homosexuality is a result of a misguided upbringing. We have proven this theory to lack any truth and scientific backing. How many more studies need to be conducted to prove our point? Conducting more studies will not change the radical Christian movement's mind. They have secured themselves behind their misinterpretation of the Bible on the subject of homosexuality. Some will always live in ignorance and stupidity. Hopefully this chapter will change your mind or build up the truth you already knew. These studies do give us more room to go forward in our research. The latest study to conclude a genetic link is found in studies of family trees and DNA. Over the last few years we have found out that DNA research has gained a lot of support, even in our courts. A team at the National Cancer Institute's Laboratory of Biochemistry reported a study they came upon while doing a study on DNA. This study was related to a study conducted by Dean Hamer. The research was printed up in Time Magazine of July 26, 1993. The researchers reported the following:

> That families of 76 gay men included a much higher proportion of homosexual male relatives than found in the general population. Intriguingly, almost all the disproportion was on the mother's side of the family. That prompted the researchers to look at the chromosomes that determine gender, known as X and Y. (p. 36 Time Magazine)

The study has added to the previous studies showing a genetic link. To date, the X Y chromosomes have brought us closer to a genetic link in homosexuality. Again, we cannot forget about the other components of hormonal, psychological, and social factors. They all play a part in the sexual orientation of a person. Therefore, we can say without a doubt that one's orientation, homosexual or heterosexual, is not a choice. Our orientation is with us from birth and enhanced in early life. In conclusion, there is growing evidence that sexual orientation on any level is not simply learned behavior.

> Each dimension of sexual orientation can be measured on a continuum, Remafedi explains. Yet rarely is a measurement identical for any two people, whether self-identified as homosexual, heterosexual or bisexual. "You could be 100 percent homosexual in your fantasies, 50 percent homosexual in your behaviors, et cetera. If you have a continuum for each of these dimensions, and they are lines intersecting at some point, finally you create a sphere. Our sexual orientations are not just one, two or three—heterosexual, homosexual or bisexual—but they are infinite permutations." (p. 62, *Passages of Pride*)

The problem comes when we seek to change something which cannot be altered. Sexuality is seen in three areas:

BEHAVIOR: Our acting out. What we do with sex. I call this BODY STUFF.

IDENTITY: Who we see ourselves to be. I call this MIND STUFF.

ORIENTATION: Who we are at the very core of our being. This I call INTERNAL STUFF.

We can change our behavior, which for the homosexual is living in the Closet (living a lie). This has proven to be very damaging to the psychological, mental and spiritual well being of a person. It takes years to remedy the situation. We can change our identity, which is our thinking. This we call brain washing, which happens a lot in religion. Studies have shown us how it affects people. It has lasting consequences, which takes years of therapy. Lastly, we look at orientation, which is the internal. Most psychologists/psychiatrists will agree that success rate in this area has been small. Dr. Richard Green, psychiatrist at the University of California, Los Angeles Medical Center, makes the following statement:

> Research data on lesbians seeking to change sexual orienta-
> tion are too sparse to offer a meaningful reply. The data on
> gay men shows that the majority who seek to change sexual
> orientation do not, either regarding fantasy or overt behavior.
> Some change behavior markedly, but fantasy minimally. A
> few case reports claim that via religious therapy or psychi-
> atric or psychological therapy, sexual reorientation of both
> fantasy and behavior has occurred. (p. 6, *Why is My Child
> Gay?*)

Those who seek change, do so because of religious teachings. In the next chapter we will look at the various therapies used by the radical Christian movement to change a homosexual's orientation. The real problem with the radical Christian movement is not the issue of change. The radical Christian movement has a rather narrow view of sexuality. It is important to bear in mind that sexuality involves much more than what a person does with their genitals/vagina. More fundamentally, it is who we are as a body—selves who experience the emotional, cognitive, physical and spiritual needs for intimate communion—human and divine. It is these areas which are damaged by the misunderstanding of human sexuality. That not all of us can be heterosexual, homosexual or bisexual. Within these three are a variance, which cannot be explained in any simple terms. We are all unique creations made by God. In the end he/she will see the creation as they had made it. For mankind to understand all that God has made would make them God. As the old question goes: Why change something which does not need fixing. Therefore, let us enjoy what God has made. The fact that homosexuality has existed since the beginning of time is the only issue at hand. Homosexuals are here to stay. No matter what the radical Christian movement seeks to do will change that fact.

There needs to be no change. It is best left alone. What a dull world it would be, if we were all the same. It is the diversity which God has created for a purpose. We have failed to find unity among God's creation. If we ever find that unity we will have arrived. Once that happens we will not exist as we do today. The end will, no doubt, have come.

Chapter 14

Those Who Get Married

In this chapter, we will look at those gays and lesbians who sought marriage as a way to cure their homosexuality. There are those who got married and realized later they were gay or lesbian. On the other hand, there are those who get married knowing their attraction for the same gender. Usually those in this category come from a religious group, which condemns homosexuality. Whatever the case, the end results are devastating. Not only does it affect the individual, but their family and friends. Getting married will not change the fact that one is a homosexual. Dr. Gary Collins says it best:

> Most researchers do agree, however, that homosexuality is no more chosen than a native language. (p. 282, *Christian Counseling*)

Another way to put it: it's like changing apples into oranges. It can't be done. The following story proves that point. In 1993 I was a guest on the Phil Donahue Show. The subject was about Ex-gay ministry and whether homosexuals could become heterosexuals. One of the guests was Colin Cook and his wife, which I shared earlier about what happened after the show. During the show Colin's wife held his arm and it seemed he had truly had a conversion experience. Throughout the show he and others said they no longer struggled with homosexuality. Their message was Jesus had helped heal their homosexuality. For someone like myself, who had been in the same type of ministry did not buy their message of a conversion experience. Because radical fundamentalism sees homosexuality as a sin, causes those struggling with their orientation to change based on misguided beliefs about homosexuality. Since the Phil Donahue Show Colin Cook has been caught in homosexual behaviors, which he denies, yet his wife has left him. It is amazing how many homosexuals get married because of society and religious reasons, yet down the road end up divorced. The sad Commentary is the damage caused. In most cases those that are religious never dawn the church again. Those who do find their way back to the church, do so through counseling and much soul searching. In Colin's case, he continues to be in denial about his homosexuality. Also continues to lead others down a path of destruction by sin, fear tactics, condemnation tactics, shame tactics and other tactics which sees homosexuality as sin. It is tactics such as the ones mentioned, that causes homosexual people to seek change through marriage. All getting married does is change the outward appearance, but does not change the orientation. Most homosexuals who get married never cease the struggle with homosexuality. The radical fundamentalist would have us believe this is the temptation the gay Christian must endure. We must answer the following question. If they were truly heterosexual from birth why the struggle with homosexuality? The answer is simple. Those homosexuals who get married do not change anything. They are still a homosexual who has simply covered up their true identity. This is the message of many gays and lesbians who have married. They believed getting married might change their feelings of being a homosexual. This does not take the problem away, but adds to the situation of denial. As more gays and lesbians come out of the closet, others will realize their sexuality. Some people know their orientation at an early age:

> Sexual orientation appears to be determined prior to adolescence and prior to homosexual or heterosexual activity. The

most important single predictor of adult homosexuality was a self-report of homosexual feelings, which usually occurred three years before genital homosexual activity. *(Psychology The Science of Behavior, p. 169).*

Most know their orientation by the time they reach their late teens. Because of society and religious views, many homosexuals repress their true feelings and substitute it for a lie. In this case, those who seek marriage to cover up their true identity in hopes of a cure. In speaking with a group of ex-married heterosexual men and women who were truly homosexual, they had this to say, "We did love our marriage partners, but were not sexually attracted to them in any fashion. The repressed feelings of homosexual attraction kept surfacing." In an effort of some sort like prayer and counseling they kept themselves in denial. This of course lead to:

-False guilt
-False shame
-Depression
-Drinking and drugging
-Sex behind closed doors
-Suicidal thoughts

Every person we spoke with talked a lot about being depressed and suicidal, which stemmed from the false guilt and shame. When all is said and done, such marriages should have never been formed. The partner also realizes in most cases that their other half is homosexual. The denial factor is present at both ends of the spectrum. It is when both partners allow the truth to be known that all hell breaks loose. When this happens, the repression is let loose and the long road to recovery can begin. Some of the damage cause by the false pretenses of marriage will never be repaired. The scars will always be felt. It will be a reminder of something that was never intended to be. A homosexual can never be a heterosexual—no matter what the situation.

Can therapy change sexual orientation? No. Even though homosexual orientation is not a mental illness and there is no scientific reason to attempt conversion of lesbians or gays to heterosexual orientation, some individuals may seek to change their own sexual orientation or that of another individual (for example, parents seeking therapy for their child). Some therapists who undertake this kind of therapy report that they have changed their client's sexual orientation (from homosexual to heterosexual) in treatment. Close scrutiny of their reports indicates several factors that cast doubt: many of the claims come from organizations with an ideological perspective on sexual orientation, rather than from mental health researchers; the treatments and their outcomes are poorly documented; and the length of time that clients are followed up after the treatment is too short. In 1990 the American Psychological Association stated that scientific evidence does not show that conversion therapy works and that it can do more harm than good. *(Answers to Your Questions About Sexual Orientation and Homosexuality*, p. 3)

All of the prayers, healing, counseling and conversions in the world will not change one's orientation, be it homosexual or heterosexual. We have seen people try to behaviorally and cognitively change their orientation, which we find is false hope and brainwashing. It never was and never will be what God intended. Getting married will not make a homosexual a heterosexual. Covering up reality does not take away the facts nor change the given situation. The greatest tragedy out of a situation like this is the children. For example, when Colin Cook went on the Phil Donahue Show to say he no longer struggled with homosexuality, which he was telling the whole world, he failed to let his children know his secret. Before the show was to air, Colin said he was going to sit with his two boys and tell them about his sinful life as a homosexual, but that God had healed him of his perverted life. Yet several years later, Dr. Ronald Lawson would uncover his secret homosexual activities, which Colin conducted while counseling ex-gays. This uncovering caused Colin's wife to see reality for what it is.

> Cook's wife told the Times that Colin had even fooled her. "I did not fully realize how difficult it was going to be," she said of his homosexual desires. "I thought it was in the past. Certainly, I should have asked a lot more questions." (*Connection* p. 7)

This is the sad story of so many people in the same situation. Colin's wife left him later that year. This is the sad commentary of those who refuse to see the truth and live in denial. Can you imagine how confused his children must be? It is denial which causes the falsehood. There is no doubt it is the children who are caught in the middle. When all is said and done everyone in the family structure suffers because no one would admit to the truth of one parent being a homosexual. The pain and suffering that will be felt by all those involved could have been prevented at the very outset. Getting married will not change a homosexual into a heterosexual. Such pretenses bring devastation to everyone involved. Again, it takes years of hard work to reverse such situations as Colin Cook's. His story is just one of many such stories. We are happy to say that many homosexuals who get out of a heterosexual marriage are able to put their lives back together. Even though they are able to go on with a much happier life, the scars of the past will never go away. Hopefully, in the future we can correct this situation, so that others do not make the same mistakes. It is time for these ex-gay ministries to find help for their own denial of their homosexuality. Their sickness need not be spread around. It is a sickness that leads to deception, denial and lies for those struggling with their ordination. This is simply not needed. God has made us all who we are—homosexual or heterosexual. It is impossible to change anyone without a negative reaction, which we have seen in this chapter. Dr. Gary Collins, who is a Christian psychologist, makes the following statement:

Change is never easy for homosexuals and their counselors. The counselee dropout rate is high and enthusiastic reports from ex-gay ministries often appear to be overly optimistic (p. 288)

Ex-gay ministries do say they see more change than what is seen in studies and observations, which see very little change, if any. The reason for this misconception comes from the Ex-gay's denial of their homosexuality. Dr. Gary Collins does see change as possible, which comes from his strong religious convictions and not from the science of psychology. Most psychologists, including myself, would disagree with Dr. Gary Collins' view. Again, you cannot change a person's orientation no more than you can change a tomato into an onion. This may seem dogmatic, but when have the radical Christians ever been reasonable? For example, Dr. Gary Collins gives a counselor some guidelines, which will help homosexuals change their orientation.

1—The counselee honestly faces his or her homosexuality.

2—The counselee has a strong desire to change.

3—The counselee is willing to break contact with homosexual companions who tempt the counselee into homosexual behavior.

4—There is a willingness to avoid drugs and alcohol since these leave one more vulnerable to temptation.

5—The counselee is able to build a close, non-sexual, intimate relationship with the counselor or other same-sex person.

6—The counselee experiences acceptance and love apart from homosexual friends and contacts.

7—The counselee is under thirty-five and/or is not deeply involved in homosexual attachments to others.

8—The counselee has a desire to avoid sin and to commit his or her life and problems to the Lordship of Jesus Christ.

This is the thinking of those professionals with a strong religious attachment. No doubt, they have been misled and misguided by their profession and religious convictions. We will answer each one of these concepts separately.

1—The fact is, most homosexuals have honestly faced who they are when they come out of the closet. Those who are lying usually are married or part of an ex-gay ministry. The radical Christian churches need to face the fact that homosexuality is not something that needs changing or can be changed. It is sad how many homosexuals are fed the idea that homosexuality is a sin or disease. This brings about false guilt, condemnation and shame. Therefore, Christian counselors need to deal with their homophobia (fear) about homosexuality.

2—Usually this desire is coupled with guilt and condemnation tactics with a religious overtone. Those who get married knowing their homosexual orientation talk a lot about these tactics, which caused them to marry.

3—If there was no such thing as homosexual orientation why worry about the temptation? If one is truly heterosexual, there is no need to worry about homosexuality. It is a fact that homosexuality is not a disease like alcoholism. This misconception is a radical Christian myth.

4—It needs to be said, that drugs and alcohol are not a homosexual problem. Drugs and alcohol are everyone's problem. It also does not turn out homosexuals.

5—All the homosexuals I know have very close intimate relationships with other same-sex persons without sex being involved. Again, a radical Christian myth, which makes gays and lesbians to be sex maniacs – this is not true.

6—Again, all homosexuals I know have experienced acceptance and love from many heterosexuals. Unfortunately, the radical Christians have missed out in the venture. It truly is a loss on their part.

7—What does age have to do with change? Oh, I remember—it's hard to teach an old dog new tricks. Once again it's a myth. Homosexuality is not taught.

8—Here is the condemnation being given by misquoted Scripture from the radical Christian's viewpoint. Homosexuality is not a sin, which has been proven in another chapter. Also, many gays and lesbians are Christians and fully embrace the Lordship of Jesus Christ. Romans 8:38-39 has become the gay Christians' verse which gives them all the hope they need in their relationship with Jesus Christ.

These eight concepts by Dr. Gary Collins have caused such devastation for those gays and lesbians who have come out of the radical Christian movement. Many seek marriage in hopes of a cure. The only cure is to know who you are, whether it be homosexual or heterosexual. Get to know that person inside and out. Accept who you are, because God made you the wonderful person you are. Once you do this you will grow to be the fine person you already are. As the

Serenity Prayer puts it: "Change those things that you can, accept those things you cannot change." Most of all, ask God for the wisdom to know the difference. Don't let anyone lead you down a destructive path. The story about Colin Cook proves this very point. May the truth you find set in these pages set you free or someone you know who may be a homosexual.

Chapter 15

Gay Youth

Our youth are our future. Today's youth are growing up fast. They are much more aware, educated and open about today's issues. Even with this growth, bigotry and hatred has not changed. No amount of awareness, education and openness can prepare one for bigotry and hatred. For years, the gay community has been held in silence by bigotry and hatred. It has been our youth who have broken the silence. In taking a stance there is always a cost. Coming out of the closet as a gay person is not easy at any age. When a young person comes out of the closet there are many added problems, such as being kicked out of their homes, forced into counseling (to change their orientation), and the list goes on. The stress, agony and hurts are tremendous. Among our youth in general, suicide has become a national problem. It is the second leading cause of death among our youth. This has caused our country to take a look at this issue, which is a real problem.

National Statistics:
-Gay and lesbian youth comprise 30% of teen suicides
-40% of youth are homeless—throwaway/runaway
-28% are high school dropouts
-50% are rejected by families
-80% report severe isolation problems

-97% of students hear anti-gay comments in school
-50% of gay men and 20% of lesbians are harassed or assaulted in secondary schools.

(Governor's Commission on Gay & Lesbian Youth, Boston, Mass. 1994; U.S. Dept. of Health & Human Services 1989). These statistics are alarming. In this chapter, we will focus upon gay youth. The radical Christian movement would have us believe the suicide rate of gay youth is because they are unhappy with who they are. This is not true. We know that most gay youth are happy with who they are and well adjusted. It is the bigotry and hatred, which mounts the problems. It has become the subject of many shows, the bigotry and hatred among minority groups (blacks, Hispanics, Jews, and homosexuals). This behavior is something we learn, therefore, it can be changed. Hopefully, we can begin to recognize bigotry and make changes that will bring unity among people. This begins with the adults, who teach their youth about bigotry. Therefore, gay youth have a lot of issues to deal with when coming out of the closet. The good news is that many gay youth are getting the support they need from each other by attending support groups for gay youth. Our youth are learning to stand together for truth. It is important for gay youth to seek support from others in the same situation. We must commend those youth that have held to their own convictions and are willing to make a statement. It is hard to stand up against bigotry. Those youth who have fallen to suicide is due to the pressure of parents, schools and churches. It is sad how the church, in particular, has played in the emotions of the youth, by piling guilt upon the innocent. The church over the years has used guilt, condemnation and damnation to change people. This is a form of brainwashing, which causes much damage to a person's well being. Most suicides among gay youth are not due to their unhappiness of being gay, it is the homophobic society which brings about suicide among growing teenagers. There are those teenagers who find out who they are at a young age. The radical Christian movement would have us believe the youth are confused and finding themselves. The problem comes when the radical Christian movement says gay youth are confused about their identity. We should never take our youth at face value. Many young people know who they are at a young age. The radical Christian movement does not help in the growth of our gay youth by confusing the issue with guilt and shame. God made gay people for the uniqueness they are. This uniqueness God does not seek to change. Nowhere in the Gospels do we see our Lord Jesus seeking to change a person for who they are (Jewish, Gentile, Black or Homosexual), but Jesus did seek to change hate to love; greed to long suffering; sadness to joy. It is those inner qualities that Jesus was concerned with. Jesus wanted the people to accept Him as the Savior who came to live, die and rise again. The issue of being gay never comes up by our Lord, because it was not an issue of discussion, but an issue of acceptance. Our youth of today are dealing with so many pressures that are beyond our imagination. The awareness of their homosexuality came early in life:

> For as long as they can remember, from five, six, seven years old, they have felt "different," say gay and lesbian youth, nothing that they could fix a label to at such an early age, yet something that set them apart and deepened as they grew into their teenage years. By early adolescence, say gay teens, they were aware of an affection for people of the same gender. (p. 1, *Passages of Pride*)

The radical Christian movement would have us believe that homosexuality is a learned behavior. Where did they learn the behavior? Most gay youth grow up in a heterosexual household, go to a heterosexual school and live in a heterosexual society. Therefore, where do they become homosexual? It's not something you catch or learn. Neil Carlson makes the following statement:

> Sexual orientation appears to be determined prior to adolescence and prior to homosexual or heterosexual activity. The most important single predictor of adult homosexuality was

a self-report of homosexual feelings, which usually occurred three years before genital homosexual activity. This finding suggests that homosexuality is a deep-seated tendency. It also tends to rule out the suggestion that seduction by an older person of the same sex plays an important role in the development of homosexuality. (p. 169, *Psychology The Science of Behavior*)

Many young gay people are told they are going through a phase and it will end. Once they get over the hurdle of raging hormones they will eventually find an attraction towards the opposite sex. When this does not happen, they begin to feel something is wrong with them. Because of the message coming from the radical Christian movement, they begin to feel they're sick or evil or immoral. This is the message which needs to be changed. Gay youth need to know they are not sick or evil or immoral for being a homosexual. Being different is not something to be ashamed of.

Adolescence is tough enough. But to suddenly put a word to their lifelong "difference," a word used so contemptuously in society—lesbian or gay—can be a wounding experience for teens. On top of all their fear and confusion, they become vulnerable targets of harassment, prejudice and hatred. (p. 1, *Passages of Pride*)

God has made us all different, therefore, the word is not something ugly. Yet, the pressure to conform is great. Many youth go into the closet. Our young people end up living a double life in order to cover up their homosexuality. Many of our youth become good at hiding who they are from family and friends. It is the closet, which causes a lot of turmoil for gay youth. There are several patterns a young boy goes through when he have a homosexual feeling.

PATTERN ONE: Rage. At puberty a young boy may have weak homosexual desires. We know that over 40% of the male population has had some type of homosexual experience. Having sex with some one of the same gender does not make a person gay. Those who do have homosexual desires at this stage indulge in a psychological game called repression and reaction formation. At this point they are fearful of their emotional and physical yearning for someone of the same sex. Automatically, they put this thought deep into their subconscious, because the radical Christians' narrow understanding of sexuality and sex brings about such reactions to young boys' discovering their sexuality. If they are truly homosexual they learn early to take on the heterosexual role. This type of confusion causes psychological ramifications, which are unhealthy.

PATTERN TWO: Terror. At this point the homosexual desires are too strong to repress. The young boy is conscious of their homosexuality, but hate it, and themselves. This hatred is due to the homophobia from society and religion. They try very hard to keep their homosexuality a secret.

PATTERN THREE: Wretched Excess. These are those who have a very strong effeminate and feminine appearance (sometimes a role they take on). In either case it is hard to conceal who they are. This is not the case for most homosexuals.

In each one of these patterns we see what homophobia causes in our adolescent boys. Some of the homophobia comes from those who are homosexual themselves, but will not accept their orientation. There are many of our youth who realize who they are as a gay person and meet the challenges ahead. Here is the story of one young man who wrote an article about himself as a gay person. This article appeared in his High School newspaper.

"Homophobia (the state of being afraid of, or anti-gay) exists at Hallandale High. As a gay teen, it affects me. For years I have denied this fact to myself, seeking change when I knew well enough that change was impossible, just as impossible as it would be for a heterosexual (straight) person to change his or her sexual preference. Thankfully, I have come to accept myself with the help of supportive parents, friends, relatives and pastors. Growing up gay in a straight world is not easy, being a minority is never easy. Day by day I sit in class hearing anti-gay remarks and feeling anti-gay sentiments from teachers as well as students. I hear negative comments from some of my best friends who have no idea that I am gay. I fear being ridiculed and losing friends if I were to openly admit my orientation (which I would very much like to do). Where do these negative attitudes come from? Parents, pastors, other friends and television all contribute. Are these people so well informed about homosexuality? Why not get the information first-hand from people who are really educated such as those who have studied human sexuality for years, or even from gay people themselves. We usually fear what we do not understand. Go to the library (public, that is) and read some of the positive gay material. What you will find is a basic agreement that homosexuality is either a biologically or environmentally caused state that naturally occurs almost everywhere in nature. A conservative estimate is that 10 percent of the population is gay. In a class of 30, there should statistically be 3 gay people. Due to societal restrictions, it is against these people's better judgement to "come out". My own personal experience may dispel some common misconceptions. Both a loving and caring mother and father raised me. I was never molested. Neither of my parents were absent, overly weak, or overly dominant. I grew up in a straight environment, in a straight society. As far back as I can remember, I have had feelings for the same sex. I have hardly ever experienced feelings for the opposite sex. I am sure of my sexuality, just as sure as most straight people are of theirs. There is no age limit. Being gay is not something you grow out of. Whoever heard of growing out of heterosexuality? I guess what I want, is to be able to freely express myself. Seeing straight couples holding hands in school or in the mall gets to me. Why can't I do that without being ridiculed and taunted? Why won't I sign my name to this? It's unfortunate, but I know that if I do sign it problems could arise that could cause friction with my friends, other students and teachers. The worst part is that I can't think of one legitimate reason for people to be against homosexuality. Tell me, if two people are in a loving, caring relationship, or are even just dating, and they happen to be of the same sex, who are they

REV. JERRY STEPHENSON, Th.D., Ph.D.   141

bothering? Who gets hurt? No one. In short, homophobia can be stopped. I am simply trying to create a better future for myself. I do not want to force the fact that I am gay on the rest of the world. However, when I hear negative comments like I hear, and feel oppression like I feel, I get the desire to do something to make a difference. Hopefully, I am getting through. The gay issue does not deserve apathy, but scrutiny, so that the uninformed, and prejudices, can be destroyed. Inform yourselves, then rethink your own opinions and values."

We must admire and honor such youth who stand for who they are spite of the odds. The greatest men and women of America fought against the odds and came out winners. This story shows the maturity of many of our gay youth who overcome homophobia and bigotry. Many of our youth have thought through the issue of being gay. At the beginning of the article it is stated that this person denied the fact that they were gay. This is an issue every gay person faces. It is sad that in a country that was built upon freedom of speech, religion and the list goes on, gays are being denied that freedom, because of who they are. If we were to take a survey and ask this question: As a straight person could we change you to be gay? The answer most undoubtedly would be no. How is it that so many straight people say that gay people can and should change? How can we say that on one hand that one cannot change (straight), but on the other hand say that one can change (gay)? This type of thinking causes confusion among our youth. They are confused enough with life and the changes they are facing on a daily basis. But as we have seen, some of our youth are very well adjusted with life. The problem with most people is their lack of knowledge about homosexuals. The information can be devastating in the wrong hands. For example, the church would have us believe that homosexual males come from a unloving father and dominant mother. Yet our story tells us otherwise. They say that homosexuals were molested, yet our story does not hold to this view. This story is just one of many who do not fit the radical Christians view of why someone is a homosexual. It is their ignorance and stupidity, which causes problems. The fact is that many gays live in the closet. Some even get married and play the heterosexual life, but have a homosexual relationship on the side. Somewhere along the way, most of them come to the realization that they are gay. When they finally come out of the closet all hell breaks loose. What is sad about a story such as this is the guilt, shame and lies which fill its pages. It is sad, what many of our youth go through before they find themselves. The mental anguish, psychological pain and spiritual damnation are lasting. It takes years for the damage to be caused. It will take a lifetime to work through the pain caused by homophobia, bigotry, hatred and lies. Today's gay youth are realizing the past mistakes of gays staying in the closet or conforming to those who do not accept homosexuality. Therefore they are realizing who they are as a person and accepting their orientation. This has not alleviated the problem of the radical Christians' views on homosexuality, which affects society's views on the subject. We can see changes occurring as people learn about homosexuality. This is a slow process, but a step forward in the right direction. Hopefully, we can bring down the suicide rate of our gay youth with this fact. Again, we are making steps forward, but it is slow. We still have a long way to go with the subject of homosexuality. Our youth are worth the battle against such groups as the radical Christian movement. Some Christian churches are seeing the truth about gays and lesbians.

There is the continued idea, that our youth are confused with their sexual orientation. We know there are some that are not sure, but with healthy education on the subject, they will no doubt come to their own conclusions. Also, there are those that continue to say that homosexuality is an illness of some sort, like mental illness or alcoholism. This concept has been repudiated by the following: The American Medical Association, American Academy of Pediatrics, American Counseling Association, the American Psychiatric Association, the American Psychological Association, the American School Health Association, the National Association of School Psychologists, and the National Association of Social Workers. What else can we do to prove this illness misconception of homosexuality? It is time to accept the facts and stop feeding into the misconception. A professor of mine once said, "We can say cows fly, but we know that cows can't fly." In the same way we can say that homosexuals can change to be heterosexuals, but we know they can't. It is time to face the facts presented and help our youth find their own place in the area of human sexuality. We can say that many youth are learning at a younger age that it is ok to be homosexual. If only we could help the radical Christian Movement and bigots of all kinds come to see the truth about homosexuality. They too, are a part of God's wonderful creation. And don't you forget about that. God loves you for the way He made you.

Chapter 16

About Studies and Surveys

Throughout this book we have sought to prove our points by way of scholars. A Scholar is one who is an expert in a specific field of study. In this chapter, we will look at a survey conducted to answer some of the questions being asked by people who are either ignorant or stupid. There have been many studies conducted on gays and lesbians. These studies have either been for or against homosexual orientation. At the beginning of this chapter we will look at some of the experts who have shed positive light upon the subject at hand. They answer the question of homosexuality being a choice or behavior. This type of thinking has been the footstool of the Radical Christian Movement. Again, as stated in earlier chapters, the exact causes of heterosexuality and homosexuality are unknown. The results of sexual orientation are likely to be the results of several factors, including genetic, hormonal, and environmental. There is no one factor that makes up one's orientation. The sick part about the Radical Christian Movement is their desire to fit people into a particular mold. Just as complex as the human element is—so is their orientation. There have been studies done with great care and professionalism, which give cause for homosexuality. Below are just some of the studies done, that give causes for homosexuality: Dr. Bailey and Dr. Richard Pillard, psychiatry professors at Boston

University School of Medicine conducted a study on twins. The study gave clues to homosexuality.

Dr. Laura Allen and Dr. Roger Gorski of the University of California concluded in their study a difference in brain structure of heterosexual and homosexual men.

Dr. Simon LeVay of the Salk Institute in LaJolla California states a region of the hypothalamus, a part of the brain that helps regulate sexual behavior was smaller in homosexual men that in heterosexual men.

Dr. Martin Reite, professor of psychiatry at the University of Colorado Health Sciences Center concluded a difference in a part of the brain between heterosexual and homosexual men.

A team at the National Cancer Institute came upon a profound link in the X Y chromosomes of gay men, which showed more of the mother's gene.

These are just some of the many studies that have shown a positive aspect of homosexuality. It is showing us there is a genetic link to the whole mystery of homosexuality. It was for this reason, that I conducted my own survey to answer some of the misguided answers coming out of the Radical Christian Movement about the causes of homosexuality.

This chapter is the result of a survey. The following survey was conducted on 67 Christian gays and lesbians:

1) Are you in or out of the closet?

2) At what age did you realize you were gay?

3) Did you grow up in a church?

4) At the time that you came to realize you were gay was your faith in God affected by the radical Christian movement?

5) Did you leave the church after coming to the realization that you were gay?

6) Were you shunned or forced out of the church when you came out as a gay person?

7) Back then, did your faith group tell you that you were going to Hell for being gay?

8) Did you suffer any psychological and spiritual ramifications from coming out to yourself about being gay?

9) Were you forsaken by family and friends for being gay?

10) Did you ever think about suicide?

11) Did you ever attempt suicide?

12) Did you ever try to change your homosexuality?

13) Have you ever received counseling for your homosexuality?

14) Was it hard coming out of the closet?

15) As a Christian, did you ever struggle with being gay?

16) Do you still suffer any scars from your past faith group's feelings about homosexuality?

17) How long has it taken you to recover spiritually and psychologically?

18) On a scale of 1 to 10 (1 being good and 10 being bad), what effect does the radical religious Christian groups have on your psychological and spiritual well-being after you had come to realize that you were gay?

This survey does not shed light on those gays and lesbians who have left the church and never returned. In this survey we look at those who have come back to the church after coming out of the closet. We will look at each question and make some observations of the results. Also, we will look at some other observations from the survey. This is a survey and not a scientific study. Hopefully at the end of the chapter we can see a pattern.

1). Are you in or out of the closet? In our survey of 67 gay and lesbian Christians, 61 of our people were out of the closet. The other 6 were still in the closet. The coming-out process is not easy and we know that many gays and lesbians take many years in coming-out. Our youth are changing this pattern. Many of our youth are coming-out at an earlier age. Whatever the time period, coming-out is not easy. Gays and Lesbians take a long time to search out their feelings about who they are. Those who come out of the closet are truly those who overcome, and are heroes.

2) At what age did you realize you were gay? The results are as follows:

3	(1)
4	(1)
5,5,5	(3)
6,6,6,6	(4)
7,7,7,7,7	(5)
8,8	(2)
9	(1)

10,10	(2)
11	(1)
12,12,12,12	(4)
13,13	(2)
14,14,14,14	(4)
15,15,15	(3)
16,16,16	(3)
17,17,17	(3)
18,18,18,18,18	(5)
19,19,19,19,19,19,19,19	(8)
20,20	(2)
21,21	(2)
22,22	(2)
23	(1)
24,24	(2)
25,25	(2)
27	(1)
28,28	(2)
30	(1)

Our study shows that most of our people realized they were gay while in their teens. This is a lot to handle at this age. A society that does not understand homosexuality adds to the problem. On top of the bigotry, is the radical Christian movement coming in the name of Jesus to condemn homosexuality. Therefore when a gay and lesbian comes out of the closet they take the chance of losing a lot. In many cases they lose family, friends, jobs and housing. Coming-out costs a person a lot. Once a gay and lesbian realizes they are gay they must deal with that information. It is a process which takes time and thought. This realization can be a shock. On top of the realization is the homophobia, which adds to the shock and fear of being found out. This fear of being found out leads some teenagers to commit suicide, because they cannot think of facing their parents and friends. Some do come out to their parents and are forced out of their home. Whatever the case, some cannot find a way out but suicide. We know that 30% of teenage suicides is due to the issue of coming-out of the closet as a gay or lesbian.

3) Did you grow up in a church? Those in our survey do attend a gay church. Our survey shows 52 who grew up in a church. The other 15 did not attend church while growing up. These statistics will have some effect on the other questions.

4) At the time that you came to realize you were gay was your faith in God affected by the radical Christian movement? The results of this question were surprising. There were 26 people who said their faith in God was affected by the radical Christian movement. The other 41 people said their faith in God was not affected by the radical Christian movement. The results might have been different, if we were to survey those gays and lesbians who grew up in the church, yet have no faith today. Our survey was conducted on people with a strong faith in God.

5) Did you leave the church after coming to the realization that you were gay? The results were even on both sides of the issue. There were 32 people who said they did leave the church. The other 35 said they did not leave. The higher number who stayed in the church came from churches that were more understanding of homosexuals. Those who came out of the fundamentalist churches did leave the church for some time. There are churches opening their doors to the gay community, in the last few years an affiliation called Atlantic Institute of Christian Churches, which is a fundamentalist group of gay, lesbian and straight churches. Their message is that Jesus loves you just as you are. That one's orientation has nothing to do with a person's salvation. The message is: "Our hope is built on nothing less, than Jesus Christ."

6) Were you shunned or forced out of the church when you came out as a gay person? The results of this question were surprising. Only 23 said they were shunned or forced out of the church. The low number could have been due to several reasons. Some of the mainline churches have begun to open their doors to gay people. A number of churches use the military philosophy of don't ask don't tell. There are

a few mainline churches, which allow openly gay people to worship at their churches. Some gay people are not open about their orientation at their place of worship. The reasons just mentioned can have an effect upon the low number of those not shunned or forced out of the church. We do know those who attend a radical fundamentalist church must remain in the closet. Those who come out must accept their homosexuality as a sin and remain celibate. Most radical fundamentalist churches encourage counseling, such as reparative therapy.

7) Back then, did your faith group tell you that you are going to Hell for being gay? The results are not surprising. Out of 67 people 48 said they were told they were going to Hell for being gay. Can you imagine the spiritual anguish a gay person goes through when told they are going to Hell? Such a message causes many of them to try and change their orientation, without success. This alone causes psychological and mental torture. It can lead one to leave the church feeling unloved, defeated, sinful and hated. These are just a few adjectives which explain the emotions experienced by those gays who cannot overcome their homosexuality. It is this type of message, which can lead one to drinking, drugs and suicide. This type of condemnation is not good for anyone's well being. Hopefully we can help change this message coming out of the radical Christian movement. The Atlantic Association of Christian Churches has begun to give hope to those Christian gays coming out of the radical Christian movement. This survey proves that point.

8). Did you suffer any psychological and spiritual ramifications from coming-out to yourself about being gay? Any type of repression and bigotry is going to cause psychological ramifications. Also our gay Christians suffered spiritual ramifications. Truly these gay Christians have overcome a lot. This type of suffering takes years of counseling and help from others in order to find healing. Their suffering happened over time. In the same manner it takes time to bring about healing. The continued repression and bigotry of the radical Christian movement does not help the matter. The fact that 41 of 26 surveyed suffer some type of psychological and spiritual ramifications from coming-out proves this very point. Therefore, we need to end the repression and bigotry. Until then, the gay community will continue to overcome and come out as winners.

9) Were you forsaken by family and friends for being gay? Our findings were half-and-half. There were 35 people who said they were forsaken by family and friends. The other side of the issue (32) said they did have support of their family and friends. This is good news. It shows a strong bond between families and friends. But the numbers of those who are forsaken by family and friends is too high. It shows a concern that needs to be dealt with. It is sad and unthinkable that someone could forsake a loved one based on orientation. It is the fear of the unknown, which causes people to do crazy things. Educating families and friends about homosexuality will help bring down these numbers. History has shown us that we will never be rid of all bigotry and hatred. One's family and friends are an important part of their wellbeing. We know a breakdown in this area can produce great havoc. Any group that stays together grows together.

10) Did you ever think about suicide? The numbers were not that different, which is a good sign. On the other hand the number of possible suicides was slightly higher. When we look back at the last 9 questions we can understand why one would think about suicide. The radical Christian movement would have us believe that the thought of suicide is due to their unhappiness of being gay. This shows their ignorance regarding the facts. Much of the problems regarding suicide is the homophobia coming out of the radical Christian movement. They hate them in the name of God. Once again they choose to play judge and jury. (38 thought of suicide/29 had no thoughts about suicide).

11) Did you ever attempt suicide? It is good to see the number of no attempts at 48, and attempts at 19. Truly gays and lesbians have come a long way in this area, despite the homophobia coming out of the radical Christian movement. No one likes to think about suicide. People can't believe that normal people become depressed and commit suicide. This is true in minority and depressed groups. Suicide is not just an issue in the gay community, but in all communities. Suicide is not a

respecter of persons. It is an issue that will not simply go away with time. Suicide happens to all people from all walks of life, and choosing not to talk about it will not make the truth go away. Suicide it is said, is a lonely way out with no way back—a permanent solution to a temporary problem. Suicide is becoming a growing problem in this country. It is growing so much among our youth, that there is a great concern for more research and answers. Nobody wants to die. People in emotional pain invariably do everything they can, everything they know how to do, to end their pain before choosing to end their lives. Among adults suicide is the tenth leading cause of death. In youth it is the second leading cause of death. In gay people it is the pain, which produces suicidal impulses. Acting on these impulses can arise from a number of different sources:

-Shame
-Guilt
-Loneliness
- Being forsaken
-A lack of emotional coping skills
-Mental illness
-Hate and bigotry (Homophobia)

Add to these factors the stress and painful events of daily life such as family, school, work, loss of job, home and substance abuse which heightens the risk of suicide. These sources do not always pinpoint those who will commit suicide. Our gay Christians who thought of suicide found hope. The pain of depression is intense, but that pain can be alleviated. Depression and repression is curable. It is a fact that depression is a big factor in suicide on any level. Over two-thirds of people with moderate-to-severe depression experience thoughts of suicide. Depression paralyzes the will, and at the deepest point of depression, a person is often too severely immobilized to take self-destructive action. But when they do get to a point of mobilization they end their life. Again, some people do not have the coping skills to deal with bigotry and hatred. The thought of family, friends and church forsaking them is painful. Those who make it through suicidal thoughts are truly survivors. The Bible says to love your neighbor as yourself. We must learn to love ourselves in order to love our neighbor. The two go together. Love is a word we use a lot, but hard to do. Yet, love is a word that goes a long way. Love is powerful and makes the world go around. If used properly it can bring about healing on many levels.

12) Did you ever try to change you homosexuality? It is not surprising that 40 out of 67 tried to change their orientation. The message has been homosexuality is sick, a sin and perverted. With this type of message who would want to be a homosexual if you knew you would be ridiculed, fired, lose family and friends, and even be killed for being found out as a homosexual. This is not exactly a life one would choose. No doubt, such a message would cause anyone to try and change at any cost. Today we know that change is not needed, recommended and cannot happen.

13) Have you ever received counseling for your homosexuality? Only 21 out of the 67 received counseling. In most cases, it is due to the message of the church. Those who go into counseling do so because a family or church member encourages them to do so. In many cases, it is damaging to the individual who tries to change something they cannot. We would encourage all of those who come out of the closet to get counseling, which would encourage them as a homosexual. Those who suffer years of being in the closet, married and repressed should seek counseling. You cannot have years of shit piled upon you before you begin to smell. The years of hurt, fear, condemnation and repression damages one's self-worth and well being. It is through counseling we find help, hope, love of ourselves, psychological and spiritual healing.

14) Was it hard coming-out of the closet? Someone once said, "The closet is the worst place for a gay and lesbian." In coming-out there is a price. History has shown us that there is a price for freedom. When a gay or lesbian comes out of the closet there is a price to pay, but freedom is worth all the pain and loss. Our survey shows 45 out of 67 peo-

ple said coming-out was hard. It takes a gay or lesbian time, sometimes years, to come out to the world. Because of the bigotry and homophobia a gay or lesbian will pay the price. The fact is that many who come out lose family, friends, jobs, housing and even their life. It is so sad that gays and lesbians must go through so much for truth. In being who they are, they must face the bigotry and hatred of those who are not willing to accept the truth. Once again, history has shown us how bigotry and hatred can silence the truth. Just ask a black, a Jew or a woman.

15) As a Christian, did you ever struggle with being gay? The results were not surprising. Only 27 out of the 67 said they did not struggle somewhere in their Christian life with being gay. The great thing is when a gay Christian searches the Scriptures on the subject. The Atlantic Association of Christian Churches has been able to answer the radical Christian movements misconceptions and misinterpretations of homosexuality. The Bible says when we know the truth it sets us free. Those within the Alliance have truly been set free from the radical Christians' misuse of Scripture against homosexuals.

16) Do you still suffer any scars from your past faith group's feelings about homosexuality? Those in this study have found their freedom through God's love and His Word. In knowing God's Word they found freedom. Out of the 67 people surveyed 43 said they do not suffer any scars from their past faith group. One person said: "Once you give it over to the Lord the burden is lifted. Healing comes when you forgive those who transgress, hate or lie against you. Only in Jesus can we find forgiveness." What a powerful statement. The truth will truly set one free.

17) How long has it taken you to recover spiritually and psychologically from the radical Christians' homophobia? The results were varied. The results prove the fact that many gays and lesbians suffer spiritually and psychologically from homophobia. Such bigotry and hatred makes a mark in a person's life. Here are the results of the survey:

0,0,0,0	(4)
1,1,1,1,1,1,1	(7)
2,2,2,2,2,2,2,2,2	(9)
3,3,3,3,3	(5)
4,4,4,4	(4)
5,5,5	(3)
7,7	(2)
8,8,8,8	(4)
10,10,10,10	(4)
13	(1)
15,15,15	(3)
18,18	(2)
20,20,20,20,20,20	(6)
25,25	(2)
lifetime	(11)

As you can see, most gays and lesbians show a year or more to recover spiritually and psychologically from homophobia. What needs to be noted is the results of the Life Time recovery. These results are not surprising. Other such groups (blacks, Jews and women) have felt the spiritual and psychological ramifications from bigotry and hatred. Therefore gays and lesbians who suffer from homophobia feel the ramifications from bigotry and hatred. The great thing about this study is the fact that many of the gays and lesbians are able to make some recovery and go on with life.

18) On a scale of 1 to 10 (1 being good and 10 being bad) what effect does the radical religious Christian Groups have on your psychological and spiritual well-being after you had come to realize that you were gay? The results are as follows:

1,1,1,1,1,1,1,1,1,1,1	(11)
2,2,2,2,2,2	(6)
3,3,3,3,3	(5)
4,4,4	(3)

```
5,5,5,5,5,5,5,5,5,5,5,5,5,5,5,5,5,5,5   (19)
6,6,6                                    (3)
7,7,7,7,7,7                              (6)
8,8,8,8,8                                (5)
9,9,9,9                                  (4)
10,10,10,10,10                           (5)
```

The results show us the effect the radical Christian groups have on the well being of those who come out of the closet as a gay or lesbian. Their bigotry, hatred and condemnation bring about repression. Our survey showed some other facts, which were not included in this chapter. Those who filled out our survey were over 21 years of age. Those who filled out the survey noted that 27 out of 67 were married at one point of their life. The survey showed that those who were married had a lot more to lose in coming out. Therefore it was not surprising, that the coming-out process was a lot longer for these people. This point shows that getting married does not change one's orientation. There are many gays and lesbians who get married because of the homophobia. Those within radical Christian churches get married in hopes to change their homosexual orientation. This type of religious pressure to change causes devastation for not only the person coming out of the closet as a gay or lesbian, but also the family (wife and children). Sometimes the damage is never mended. The years of living a lie causes such devastation that can never be put back together. This alone should never be. Hopefully, the results of this survey will show us what can happen through homophobia. The bigotry and hatred by the radical Christian movement cause much psychological and spiritual damage to a person's well being. The recovery can take a lifetime. Those who do recover are no doubt heroes. They have truly overcome the bigotry and hatred caused by homophobia. This chapter shows us those who have fought the fight against homophobia and come out winners. On the other side of the issue it shows us the work needed to end homophobia it also shows the effects of homophobia. Hopefully, this chapter will bring about hope and healing for gays and lesbians.

Conclusion

The title of the book, *Out of the Closet and Into The Light*, says it all. I once saw a cartoon where a gay man is starting a new job and he is being guided to his new office by an employee who says "we don't discriminate against homosexuals," just as the man is led into the closet. That is what many businesses do in their actions towards gays and lesbians. They say one thing, yet their actions say the opposite. There are many that say they don't hate homosexuals or discriminate against them, they just hate their lifestyle. The radical Christian Movement says we love the sinner, but hate the sin. Both of these are contradictions in themselves, If they hate something, or sin, then a person has to hate themselves, because there is always something we do not like about ourselves or the fact that we are all sinners according to the Bible (Romans 3:23). Hopefully, the image of the cartoon got your attention. Also, it has some humor to its concept. Humor helps ease the pain that is caused by bigotry, hatred and lies against any minority group, such as gays and lesbians. A former Southern Baptist minister made the following statement, which forms the basis of this whole book.

> We who are gay, former ministers and alienated from our own denomination pray daily that some in our own community of faith will demonstrate similar courage in dispensing with the barrage of homophobic rhetoric based on ignorance of Scriptures and fear of the unknown and, instead, major on rebuilding community.

This book has focused upon the radical Christian movement, which we have seen, has influenced Western society on the issue of homosexuality.

Chris Glaser in his book, *Uncommon Calling*, says it best about some Christians' statements about gay and lesbian Christians:

> Usually, for most gay women and men, coming out in the church has meant coming out of the church...Coming out of the closet, a process the church should be enabling and ennobling, is a process which must be experienced more often in the secular world rather than the Christian community... And for most of those numerous gay persons who choose not to come out in the church because they want to stay in the church—in Christian community—the church has meant more than just a closet...the church has become for them a giant tomb, smelling of death rather than life.

It is sad to say that the radical Christian movement has failed to preach, teach and live the Scriptures regarding God's love. The Gospel Message is about Jesus. The message of God's love and forgiveness has nothing to do with one's gender, age, color or sexual orientation. Yet, the radical Christian movement continues their rhetoric about the sinful, awful, deviant and perverted lifestyle of homosexuality. It is no wonder that some gays and lesbians have no time for religion. Western society has not fared much better, until recently. The misconceptions about gays and lesbians has lasting results. For example, many gays and lesbians who have been mocked, beaten, hated and lied about suffer spiritually and psychologically. There is no doubt that such homophobia leads to such things as low self-esteem, drugs/alcohol abuse and even suicide. The radical Christian movement has sought to condemn, instead of love, the homosexual. In loving, that means to accept that person for who and what they are. Anything that seeks to tear down is not good for one's own spiritual and psychological well being. This book has shown how much work it takes to bring about spiritual and psychological wholeness to those who have been condemned. In many cases, the work is a lifetime process. Homophobia brings about false guilt and fear, just to name two. It is not positive reinforcement in a person's life. There is no benefit to this type of reaction. Such behavior affects not only gays and lesbians, but also their family and friends.

This book has sought to shed light on the myths regarding homosexuality. We have sought to show where these myths come from, and how damaging they are to gays and lesbians. We have looked at the issue of homosexuality from its past, present and future. Hopefully, this book has enlightened the ignorance of many. The goal of this book has been to look at the psychological and spiritual damage caused by the radical Christian movement towards its views about homosexuality. Most of all this book was written to give answers to gays, lesbians their family and friends.

The key to any myth is education. Unfortunately, there are those who will not accept truth. It is those types of people who are no longer ignorant, but stupid. Because they refuse to see the truth about any particular group, their stupidity is noted. There are those in the radical Christian movement who are truly ignorant on the issue of homosexuality. Hopefully through books such as this one they are educated on the subject. Through education they can let go of their fear regarding gays and lesbians. It is truth that will set anyone free from ignorance. For the gay person they can begin to separate the myths from the truth regarding homosexuality. Having this information can be very helpful in the coming-out process for gays and lesbians. We saw how high the suicide rate was among our gay youth. Also, how many gays and lesbians try to change their orientation? Having this book at their fingertips will help them deal with the radical Christians' misunderstanding, bigotry, hatred and lies. Unfortunately, many gays and lesbians do not see the need for religion in their lives. It does not surprise us, since such groups have pushed them out of their churches. Hopefully, such groups as The Atlantic Association of Christian Churches, mentioned earlier will help change this feeling. Gays and lesbians need to know that God loves them for who they are. The belief that homosexuality is a choice is not only false, but is damaging to those who try to change their orientation. It has been shown that homosexuals cannot change their orientation. Those who have tried to change have done so based upon a misguided belief that homosexuality is a sin. In the book we share many stories of those who have tried to change their homosexuality through counseling, marriage and other means. In every case we see the psychological and spiritual damage caused by such means. Only with the facts presented in this book, can one find freedom from the radical Christians' misinformation. It is time to set the record straight. In this age we can no longer allow ignorance and stupidity to run wild. The bigotry, hatred and lies coming out of the radical Christian churches about homosexuality must stop. The chapters in this book are filled with a lot of information and facts. In reading this book, hopefully you found the truth you may or may not want. Remember, the truth will set you free. After this book, you can no longer see gays and lesbians in the same light. I believe this book will bring you hope, if you are gay. If you are a family member or friend of someone gay, hopefully you have learned something new about your loved-one. Whatever is the reason for you reading this book, may it change you in a positive way.

Bibliography

Alexander, Christopher J. *Gay and Lesbian Mental Health*. New York: Harrington Park Press, 1996.

Allport, Gordon W. *The Nature of Prejudice*. Meneo: Addison-Wesley Publishing Company, 1979.

America Bible Society, *Nothing Can Separate Us From The Love of God*. Broadway: American Bible Society, 1976.

Andrews, Nancy. *Family: A Portrait of Gay and Lesbian America*. New York: Harper Collins Publishers, 1994.

Arterburn, Jerry, *How Will I Tell My Mother?* Nashville: Thomas Nelson Publishers, 1988.

Barker, William P., *Everyone in the Bible*. Westwood: Flaming H. Revell Company, 1966.

Baldurn, Stanley C. *What Did Jesus Say About That?* Wheaton: Victor Books (A Division of SP Publications), 1975.

Barnhouse, Ruth, *Male and Female Christian Approaches to Sexuality*. New York: The Seabury Press, 1976.

Barteck, Lynn, *Enduring Issues in Sociology*. San Diego: Greenhaven Press, 1995.

Basow, Susan, *Gender Stereotypes*. Pacific Grove: Brooks/Cole Publishing, 1988.

Bawer, Bruce, *A Place at the Table*. New York: Simon & Schuster, 1993.

Beach, Frank A. *Sex and Behavior*. Huntington: Robert E. Krieger Publishing Company, 1974.

Beach, W.R., *Dimensions in Salvation*. Washington: Review and Herald Publishing Association, 1963.

Bell, Alan P. *Homosexualities*. New York: Simon and Schuster, 1978.

Bell, Alan P., *Sexual Preference*. Bloomington: Indiana University Press, 1981.

Bender, David, *Human Sexuality: Opposing Viewpoints*. San Diego: Greenhaven Press, 1995.

Bender, David, *Teenage Sexuality*. St. Paul: Greenhaven Press, 1988.

Berkhof, Louis, *Systematic Theology*. Grand Rapids: Wm.B.

Eerdmans Publishing Company, 1941.

Blackwood, Evelyn, *Anthropology and Homosexual Behavior*. New York: The Haworth Press, 1986.

Blair, Ralph, *An Evangelical Look at Homosexuality*. New York: HCCC Inc. 1972.

Blauvelt, Livingstone, Bibliotheca Sacra, *Does the Bible Teach Lordship Salvation?* January/March 1986.

Blumenfeld, Warren J. *Looking at Gay and Lesbian Life*. Boston: Beacon Pres, 1988.

Boswell, John, *Christianity, Social Tolerance and Homosexuality*. Chicago: The University of Chicago Press, 1980.

Boyden, Jo., *Families*. New York: Gaia Books, 1993.

Bozett, Frederick, *Homosexuality and Family Relations*. New York: The Haworth Press, 1990.

Brawley, Robert L., *Biblical Ethics and Homosexuality*. Louisville: Westminister John Knox Press, 1996.

Brown, Raymond E., *The Gospel According to John I-XII*. Garden City: Doubleday & Company, Inc., 1966.

Bruce, F.F. *Jesus: Lord & Savior*. Downers Grove: Intervarsity Press, 1986.

Bull, Jennie Boyd, *AIDS: Is it God's Judgment*. Los Angeles: UFMCC Commission on Faith, Fellowship and Order, 1980.

Buttrick, George Arthur, *The Interpreter's Bible*. New York: Abingdon Press, 1952.

Chandler, Kurt, *Passages of Pride*. New York: Random House, 1995.

Christensen, F.M., *Pornography The Other Side*. New York: Praeger Publishers, 1990.

Clark, Don, *Loving Someone Gay*. New York: NAL Penguin Inc., 1977.

Clinard, Marshall B. *Sociology of Deviant Behavior*. New York: Holt, Rinehart and Winston, 1979.

Collins, Gary R. *Christian Counseling*. Dallas: Word Publishing, 1988.

Comiskey, Andrew, *Pursuing Sexual Wholeness*. Santa Monica: Desert Stream Ministries, 1988.

Comstock, Gary David. *Violence Against Lesbians and Gay Men*. New York: Columbia University Press, 1991.

Cook, Colin, *Homosexuality An Open Door*. Boise: Pacific Press Publishing Assoc., 1985.

Church, Leslie F. *Matthew Henry Commentary*. Grand Rapids: Zondervan Publishing House, 1960.

Dalton, Harlon L., *AIDS and The Law*. New Haven: Yale University Press, 1987.

DeCecco, John P., *Sex Cells and Same-Sex Desire*. New York: Harrington Park Press, 1995.

DeHann, M.R., *Studies in First Corinthians*. Grand Rapids: Zondervan Publishing House, 1956.

Diamant Louis, *Male and Female Homosexuality*. Washington: Hemisphere Publishing Corporation, 1987.

DuBay, William H. *Gay Identity*. Jefferson: McFarland & Company, 1987.

Duberman, Martin, *Cures*. New York: Dutton Books, 1991.

Dynes, Wayne R. *Encyclopedia of Homosexuality*. New York: Garland Publishing, 1990.

Eastman, Donald, *Homosexuality Not a Sin/Not a Sickness*. Los Angeles: UFMCC, 1990.

Edwards, George R. *Gay/Lesbian Liberation*. New York: The Pilgrim Press, 1984.

Ellis, Albert, *Clinical Applications of Rational-Emotive Therapy*. New York: Plenium Press, 1985.

Fairchild, Betty, *Now That You Know*. San Diego: A Harvest/HBJ Book, 1979.

Farrar, F. W. *The Pulpit Commentary*. Grand Rapids: Wm. B. Eardmans Publishing House, 1958.

First, Michael B. *DSM-IV*. Washington: American Psychiatric Association, 1994.

Fisher, Peter. *The Gay Mystique*. New York: Stein and Day Publishers, 1972.

Ford, W. Harschell, *Simple Sermons on Great Christian Doctrines*. Grand Rapids: Zonderval Publishing House, 1951.

Fortunato, John E. *AIDS the Spiritual Dilemm*a. San Francisco: Harper & Row Publishers, 1987.

Friedman, Richard C. *Male Homosexuality*. New Haven: Yale University Press, 1988.

Garnets, Linda D., *Psychological Perspectives on Lesbian and Gay Male Experience*s. New York: Columbia University Press, 1993.

Gaebelein, Frank E. *The Expositor's Bible Commentary*. Grand Rapids: Zondervan Publishing House, 1981.

Gangel, Kenneth, *The Gospel and the Ga*y. Nashville/New York: Thomas Nelson Inc., 1978.

Geller, Thomas, *Bisexuality A Reader and Sourceboo*k. Ajai: Time Change Press, 1990.

Getz, Gene A. *A Profile For a Christian Life Styl*e. Grand Rapids: Zondervan Publishing House, 1978.

Girod, Gordon H., *The Way of Salvatio*n. Grand Rapids: Baker House, 1978.

Glaser, Chris, *Uncommon Calling*. San Francisco: Harper & Row, 1988.

Goldman, Ronald and Juliette, *Children's Sexual Thinking*. Boston: Routledge & Kegan Paul Ltd., 1982.

Gouke, Mary Noel, *One-Parent Children: The Growing Minorit*y. New York: Garland Publishing Inc., 1990.

Grear, Nora Richhter, *The Creation of Shelte*r. Washington: The American Institute of Architects Press, 1988.

Gromacki, Robert R. *Salvation Is Foreve*r. Chicago: Moody Press, 1973.

Harry, Joseph, *Gay Children Grow U*p. Westport: Greenwood Press, 1982.

Heron, Ann *Two Teenagers in Twenty*. Boston: Alyson Publications Inc., 1994.

Henery, Matthew, *Matthew Henery Commentary*. Grand Rapids: Zondervan Publishing House, 1977.

Hite, Shere, *The Hite Report on Male Sexuality*. New York: Alfred A. Knopf Inc., 1981.

Hunter, Rodney J., *Dictionary of Pastoral Care and Counseling*. Nashville: Abington Press, 1990.

Imber-Black, Evan, *Secrets in Families and Family Therapy*. New York: W.W. Norton and Company, 1993.

Jacquart, Danielle, *Sexuality and Medicine in the Middle Ages*. Princeton: Princeton University Press, 1988.

Johnson, Becca Cowan, *For Their Sake: Child Abuse*. Martinsville: American Camping Association, 1992.

Johnston, Maury, *Gays Under Grace*. Nashville: Winston-Derek Publishers, 1983.

Jones, Clinton R., *What About Homosexuality?* Nashville: Thomas Nelson, 1972.

Jonsen, Albert R., *The Social Impact of AIDS in the United States*. Washington: National Academy Press, 1993.

Jordan, Winthrop D., *White Over Black: American Attitudes Toward Negro 1550-1812*. New York: W.W. Narton & Company, 1968.

Jughes, Robert B., *Everyman's Bible Commentary*. Chicago: Moody Press, 1983.

Kaetz, James P., *The Phi Kappa Phi Journal, Volume 75. No 3.* 1995.

Katchadourian, Herant A., *Human Sexuality*. Los Angeles: University of California Press, 1979.

Karlen, Arno, *Sexuality and Homosexuality*: A New View. New York: W.W. Norton & Company, 1971.

Kayal, Philip M. *Bearing Witness*. Boulder: Westview Press, 1993.

Kennedy, Elizabeth, *Boots of Leather, Slippers of God: The History of a Lesbian Community*. New York: Penguin Books, 1993.

Kinsey, Alfred C., *Sexual Behavior In The Human Male*. Philadelphia: W.B. Saunders Company, 1948.

Kirk, Marshall, *After The Ball*. New York: Doubleday, 1989.

Koertge, Noretta, *Philosophy and Homosexuality*. New York: Harrington Park Press, 1995.

Kronemeyer, Robert, *Overcoming Homosexuality*. New York: Macmillan Publishing, 1980.

Lefrancois, Guy R., *Adolescents*. Belmont: Wadsworth Publishing Company, 1976.

Leonard, Arthur S., *Sexuality and the Law*. New York: Garland Publishing, 1993.

Lewis, Sasha Gregory, *Sunday's Women*. Boston: Beacon Press, 1979.

Licata, Salvatore J., *Historical Perspectives on Homosexuality*. New York: Haworth Press, 1985.

Lincoln, C. Eric, Race, *Religion and the Continuing American Dilemma*. New York: Hill and Wang, 1984.

MacArthur, John, *The Gospel According to Jesus*. Grand Rapids: Zondervan Publishing House, 1989.

Marmor, Judd, *Homosexual Behavior A Modern Reappraisal*. New York: Basic Books, 1986.

Mass, Lawrence D., *Homosexuality and Sexuality*. New York: Harrington Park Press, 1990.

Mass, Lawrence D., *Homosexuality as Behavior and Identity, Volume II*. New York: Harrington Park Press, 1990.

Masters William H., Johnson Virginia E., *Homosexuality in Perspective*. Boston: Little, Brown and Company, 1979.

Masters, William H., Johnson Virginia A., *Master's and Johnson on Sex and Human Loving*. Boston: Little, Brown and Company, 1982.

McCuen, Gary E., *Homosexuality and Gay Rights*. Hudson: Gary McCuen Publications, 1993.

McCoy, Kathleen, *Coping with Teenage Depression*. New York: New American Library, 1982.

McNeil, John J., *The Church and the Homosexual*. Boston: Beacon Press, 1988.

Meyer, F.B., *Five Musts of the Christian Life*. Chicago: Moody Press, 1927.

Moberly, Elizabeth R., *New Perspectives on Homosexuality*. Paramount: Tamco Ministries, 1985.

Morris, William, *The American Heritage Dictionary*. Boston: Houghton Mifflin Company, 1980.

Myers, Gerald, *Evolution of AIDS*. Los Alamos National Laboratory, 1991.

Myris, Charles, *The Ryrie Study Bible*. Chicago: Moody Press, 1978.

Nava, Michael, Created Equal: *Why Gay Rights Matter to America*. New York: St. Martin's Press, 1994.

Nelson, James B. *Embodiment*. Minneapolis: Augsburg Publishing House, 1979.

Nicolosi, Joseph, *Reparative Therapy of Male Homosexuality*. Northvale: Jason Aronson Inc., 1991.

Ortez, Juan C., *Call to Discipleship*. Plainfield: Logos International, 1975.

Paine, Thomas, *Thoughts on Religion*. Virginia: University Press of Virginia, 1995.

Pennington, Sylvia, *Good News For Modern Gays*. Hawthorne: Lambda Lite Productions, 1985.

Perry, Troy D., *Don't Be Afraid Anymore*. New York: St. Martin's Press, 1990.

Petrovsky, A.V., *A Concise Psychological Dictionary*. New York: International Publishers, 1987.

Plant, Richard, *The Pink Triangle*. New York: Henry Holt and Company, 1986.

Price, Frederick, *Homosexuality: State of Birth or State of Mind?* Tulsa: Harrison House, 1989.

Rathus, Spencer, *AIDS*. Fort Worth: Harcourt Brace Jovanovich College Publishers, 1993.

Reinisch, June M., *The Kinsey Institute New Report on Sex*. New York: St. Martin's Press, 1990.

Reiss, Ira L., *An End To Shame*. Buffalo: Prometheus Books, 1990.

Rice, John R., *When a Christian Sins*. Chicago: Moody Press, 1954.

Richards, Jeffrey, *Sex, Dissidence and Damnation*. New York: Routhledge, 1990.

Ronch, Judah L., *The Counseling Sourcebook*. New York: The Crossroad Publishing, 1994.

Ruitenbeek, Hendrik M. *The New Sexuality*. New York: New Viewpoints, 1974.

Ruse, Michael, *Homosexuality*. New York: Basil Blackwell Inc., 1988.

Russell, Paul, *The Gay 100.* New York: A Citadel Press Book, 1995.

Ryrie Charles, *Balancing the Christian Life.* Chicago: Moody Press, 1975.

Schaeffer, Frances A., *The Mark of the Christian.* Illinois: Inter-Varsity Press, 1970.

Schulman, Sarah, *My American History.* New York: Routledge, 1994.

Schur, Edwin M., *Crimes Without Victims.* Englewood: Prentice-Hall, 1965.

Seymour, Richard A., *The Gift of God.* Tampa: Grace Pug Company, 1974.

Sherman, Suzanne, *Lesbian and Gay Marriage.* Philadelphia: Temple University Press, 1992.

Sherwood, Zalmon O., *Kairos.* Boston: Alyson Publications, 1987.

Springer, Sally P., *Left Brain, Right Brain.* San Francisco: W.H. Freeman and Company, 1981.

Stoudemire, Alan, *Human Behavior.* Philadelphia: Lippincott-Raven Publishers, 1997.

Tenney, Merrill C., *The Zondervan Pictorial Encyclopedia of the Bible.* Grand Rapids: Zondervan Publishing House, 1976.

The Journal of Pastoral Care Vol. 50 No. 1, Spring, 1996.

The Practice and Ethics of Sexual Orientation Conversion Therapy Journal of Consulting & Clinical Psychology. Vol. 2 pages 221-227, April 1994.

Thielicks, Helmut, *The Ethics of Sex.* New York: Harper & Row, 1964.

Tripp, C.A., *The Homosexual MATRIX.* New York: A meridian Book, 1987.

van den Aardweg, Gerard J.M., *Homosexuality and Hope*. Ann Arbor: Servant Books, 1985.

van den Aardweg,Gerard J.M., *On The Origins and Treatment of Homosexuality*. New York: Praeger Publishing, 1986.

Voth, Harold M., *Families The Future of America*. Chicago: Regnery Gateway, 1984.

Walvoord, John F., *Major Bible Themes*. Grand Rapids: Zondervan Publishing House, 19784.

Weinstein, Estelle, *Sexuality Counseling*. Pacific Grove: Brooks/Cole Publishing, 1988.

Weiss, G.C., *On Being a Real Christian*. Nebraska: Back to the Bible Publisher, 1951.

Westheimer, Ruth K., *Dr. Ruth's Encyclopedia of Sex*. New York: The Jerusalem Publishing House, 1994.

Westheimer, Ruth. *Sex and Morality*. Boston: Harcourt Brace Jovanovich Publishers, 1988.

White, Mel, *Stranger at the Gate*. New York: Simon and Schuster, 1994.

Witt, Lynn, *Out in All Directions*. New York: Warner Books, 1995.

Wolinshy, Marc, *Gays and the Military*. Princeton: Princeton University Press, 1993.

Wooden, Wayne S., *Men Behind Bars*. New York: Plenum Press, 1982.

0-595-14551-5